GREAT WORKS OF
JAPANESE
GRAPHIC ART
Douglas Mannering

A Compilation of Works from the
BRIDGEMAN ART LIBRARY

SIENA

Japanese Graphic Art

This edition first published in 1995 by
Parragon Book Service Ltd
Units 13-17 Avonbridge Industrial Estate
Atlantic Road
Avonmouth
Bristol BS11 9QD

ISBN 0 75250 723 0

Printed in Italy

Editors: Barbara Horn, Alexa Stace, Alison Stace, Tucker Slingsby Ltd and
Jennifer Warner.
Designers: Robert Mathias and Helen Mathias
Picture Research: Kathy Lockley

The publishers would like to thank Joanna Hartley at the
Bridgeman Art Library for her invaluable help.

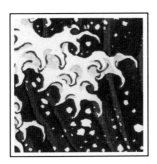

Japanese Graphic Art

Most of the Japanese arts, including painting, ceramics and lacquerwork, are at least a thousand years old. By contrast, the graphic art for which Japan is famous – the woodblock print, astonishing in its strength, elegance and colour – has been in existence for little more than two hundred years. Appropriately, it was consciously 'modern' in its own day and since the great advantage of the print is that it can be multiplied, it was also a popular art, contrasting strongly with the aristocratic exclusiveness associated with oriental painting.

Essentially, a print was made by transferring the artist's original design on to a wooden block from which many impressions could be taken. A skilled engraver cut away parts of the block, leaving on the surface only the areas that were to be printed; it was then inked and the print was taken by pressing a sheet of paper onto the block. The process could be repeated many times. The single-colour print (usually black on white) was known and occasionally practised even in medieval Japan. Printing in several colours was technically much more difficult, involving the use of a different block for each, and only in 1765 were the first multi-colour prints produced. The flowering of artistic genius that followed was all the more extraordinary in that almost all the great masters of the medium were born before 1800.

Prints in this tradition are usually classified as *ukiyo-e* or 'pictures of the floating world'. The phrase might equally well be translated as 'the passing show', since it described the glamorous, ever-changing world of city pleasures and fashions. The most pleasure-loving of the cities was Edo (present-day Tokyo), where a long period of internal peace had seen the rise of an affluent middle class with money to spend but no defined social or political role. Consequently its members gravitated towards the Yoshiwara, Edo's red-light district, which became celebrated for providing a variety of fleshly and other entertainments.

This was the milieu which the *ukiyo-e* artists immortalized. Their prints were lively and topical, appealing to those who frequented the Yoshiwara and, probably, to those who only wished they could. The most popular subject of all was beautiful women most often, though not always, the courtesans and humbler but still alluring professionals; only an occasional artist such as Utamaro also portrayed the girls who prowled the riverbank in search of customers.

The other subject of *ukiyo-e* was equally glamorous – the Kabuki theatre, which put on violent, colourful melodramas, a world away from the aristocratic Noh theatre. Its most popular performers were the idols of their audiences and, as such, obvious subjects for 'pin-up' prints.

During the 19th century the scope of the Japanese print was widened, so much so that it is stretching the term to describe masters like Hokusai and Hiroshige as *ukiyo-e* artists. Their great contribution was to popularize the landscape as a genre that not only included pure studies of nature but also everyday scenes of town and country life in many parts of Japan. Another great innovator, Kuniyoshi, virtually created his own audience for his epic, dynamic warrior prints.

Japan remained a closed society until the 1850s, when American pressure forced the country to resume contact with the West, forbidden for over two hundred years. By the beginning of the Meiji era (1868-1912), Japan was making strenuous efforts to acquire western technological expertise. One of the victims of the process was the traditional Japanese print, possibly 'outdated' in spirit and certainly ill-equipped to compete with new media such as photography. By the 1890s it had effectively passed away. Later, printmaking would undergo an impressive revival but as a rather different kind of art form.

The popular, mass-produced nature of *ukiyo-e* prints had led the Japanese to undervalue them; but when they reached the West in the mid-19th century, their fluent outlines, large areas of flat colour and daring compositional effects delighted and influenced artists such as Degas and Van Gogh. Eventually western enthusiasm inspired deeper consideration on the part of the Japanese themselves and prints took their place among the country's most cherished arts.

▷ Raiko and Shuten-doji
Moronobu (died 1694)

THE HISTORY OF PRINTS in the popular *ukiyo-e* style effectively begins with Hishikawa Moronobu. The son of a textile craftsman, he left his native Hoda for Edo (Tokyo) at some point in the 1660s. Within a decade or so he had become celebrated for book illustrations and also for his prints, issued and purchased as independent works of art. All Moronobu's work was done with black ink on white sheets, although collectors subsequently coloured some of them by hand. Raiko was the nickname of a real historical character, Minamoto no Yorimitsu, famous for his suppression of banditry in the late 10th century. In Japan the lives of such men tended to pass over into legend and so the bandits became supernatural foes and Raiko was turned into a mythical hero. His most dangerous enemy was said to have been a huge, flesh-eating monster called the Shuten-doji; Raiko and his retainers gained admittance to the beast's lair by posing as merry monks, made him drunk and cut off his head, prominently displayed in this print.

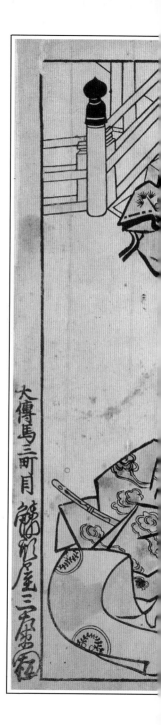

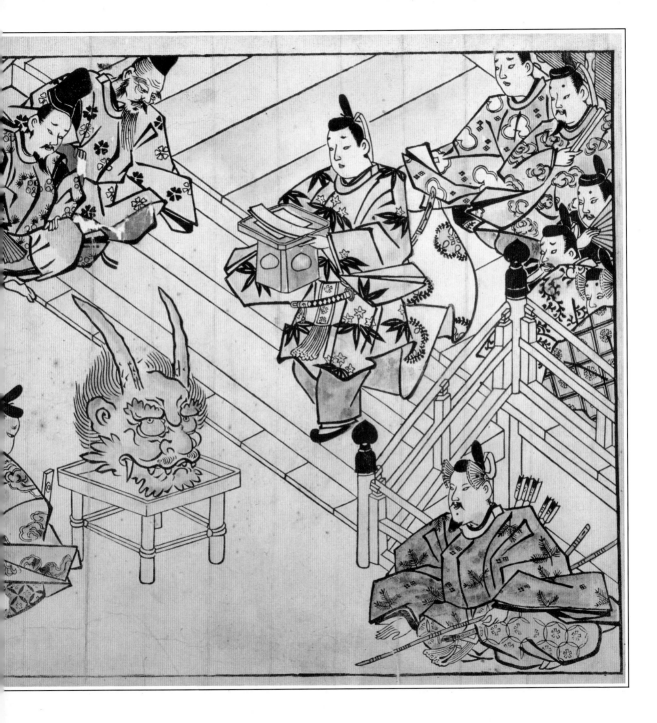

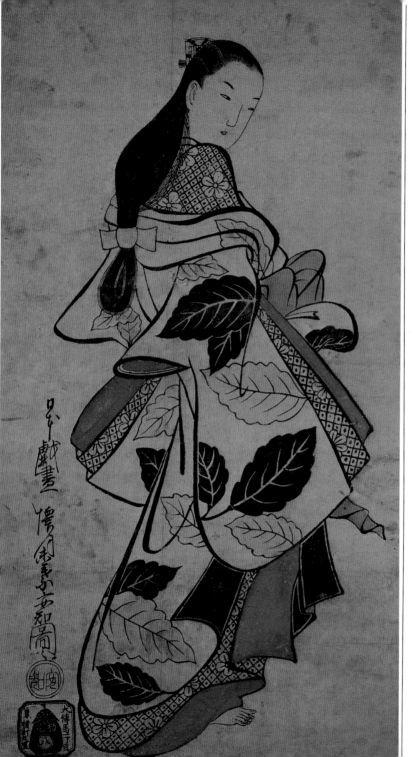

◁ **Standing Courtesan**
Anchi (active c.1700-1720?)

THE KAIGETSUDO SCHOOL, to which Anchi belonged, numbered half a dozen artists, with Kaigetsudo Ando as their master. Primarily painters, they produced only a handful of prints; but these were immensely influential, since they largely established the pictorial image of the Japanese courtesan as an aloof, queenly figure. It has been suggested that Anchi was Ando's son, and this seems all the more likely in view of the fact that *Standing Courtesan* is a near-identical copy of a painting by Ando (who issued no prints under his own name). The main changes illustrate the difference between the two mediums. The shading on the kimono has disappeared, the original pattern has been replaced by a bold leaf design, and although a few areas have been hand-coloured, the undergarment is indicated by a pattern of squares and flowers. The result is to produce a different balance between figure and decoration; Anchi's courtesan is less sumptuous and elegant but also more solid and human.

▷ The Love Letter
Masonobu (c.1686-1764)

THIS TENDER SCENE was the work of Okamura Masonobu, one of the most influential masters of the *ukiyo-e* print. During his long lifetime, techniques and subjects associated with this popular art form were still in the making and Masonobu either introduced or developed several of them. He appears to have been self-taught, and by temperament self-sufficient, since he ran his own publishing house and composed the texts for many of the albums and books he illustrated. He lived to see black-and-white works supplemented by hand-coloured prints (mostly the orange-red type shown here), and then by early two-colour prints; he died only the year before the introduction of full-colour printing. Masonobu's work has the lightness, verve and irreverence of the new city-based art; here, the swirling lines and slender, almost dancing figures are reminiscent of the western Art Nouveau style that Japanese prints were to influence over a century later.

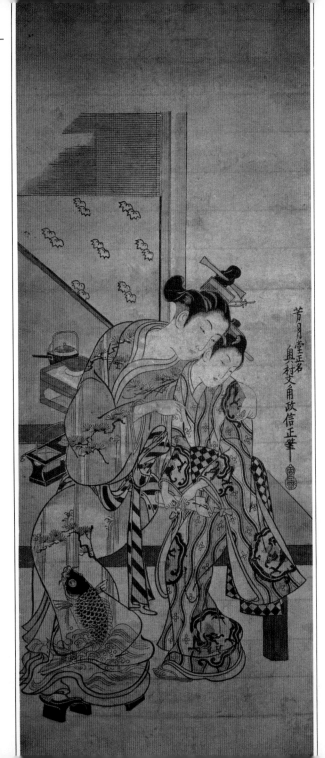

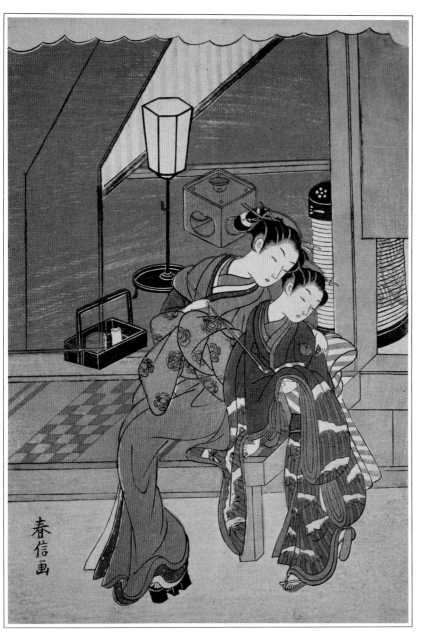

◁ **Courtesan with her Attendant**
Harunobu (c.1725-1770)

IN AN AGE of great print artists, Suzuki Harunobu is considered by many experts to have been the greatest of them all. He did have one important advantage over earlier masters: full-colour printing was developed five years before his death, and he was able to create hundreds of works of previously unattainable brilliance. However, there was more than this to his success, as can be seen in *Courtesan with her Attendant*, in which Harunobu manages to combine stylization and brilliant patterning with a strong sense of human intimacy. The most influential of all his creations was an entirely new female type – small-headed, sweet, fragile and willowy – that was all the rage for at least two decades. He also widened the scope of the *ukiyo-e*, city-pleasures style, picturing street scenes in Edo and portraying 'ordinary' girls outside the bordello, including the celebrated beauties who worked in fashionable teahouses and shops.

> **The Courtesan Mandayo and her Kamuro** c.1775
Koryusai (active c.1765-c.1784)

ISODA KORYUSAI belonged by birth to the *samurai* (military) class but renounced his rank and became a painter; he probably trained in the classic Kano style before turning to printmaking in the popular contemporary-life style of *ukiyo-e*. As the friend and chief disciple of Harunobu (page 12), he lived in the great artist's shadow even after Harunobu's early death in 1770, creating women of a similarly fragile beauty. His most distinctive work was done in long, narrow 'pillar prints', whose awkward shape he filled with remarkable skill. The most celebrated and sought-after courtesans employed *kamuro*, maids or attendants who were taken on as children; they often wore identical costumes that served as a kind of livery. Eventually they too would join the ranks of ladies of pleasure, though somewhat further down the social-sexual scale than their mistresses.

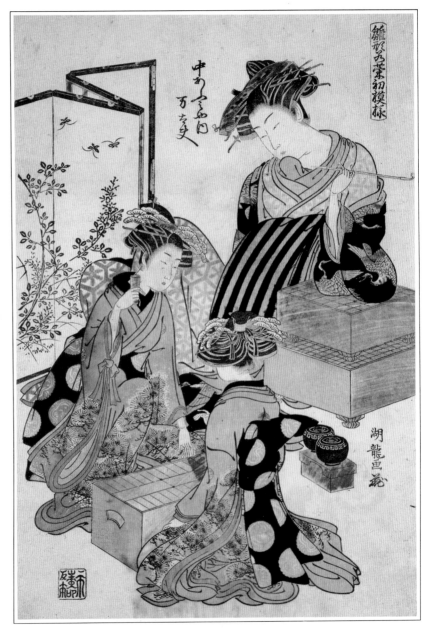

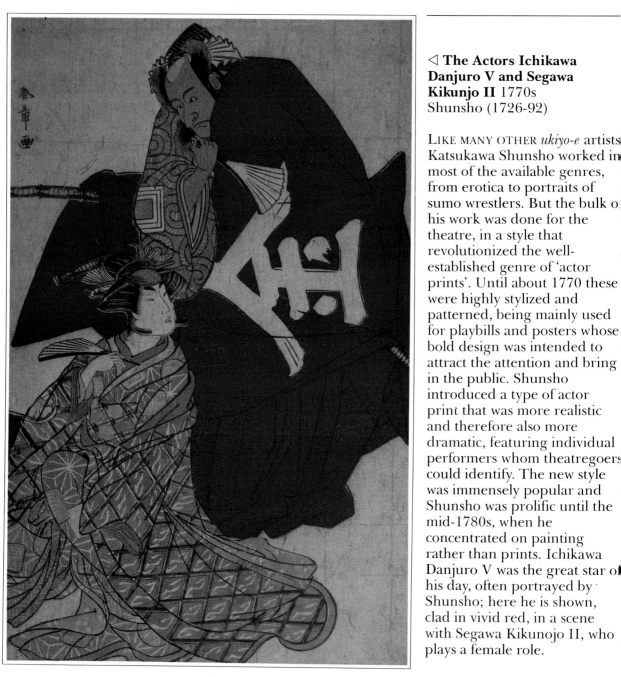

◁ **The Actors Ichikawa Danjuro V and Segawa Kikunjo II** 1770s
Shunsho (1726-92)

LIKE MANY OTHER *ukiyo-e* artists, Katsukawa Shunsho worked in most of the available genres, from erotica to portraits of sumo wrestlers. But the bulk of his work was done for the theatre, in a style that revolutionized the well-established genre of 'actor prints'. Until about 1770 these were highly stylized and patterned, being mainly used for playbills and posters whose bold design was intended to attract the attention and bring in the public. Shunsho introduced a type of actor print that was more realistic and therefore also more dramatic, featuring individual performers whom theatregoers could identify. The new style was immensely popular and Shunsho was prolific until the mid-1780s, when he concentrated on painting rather than prints. Ichikawa Danjuro V was the great star of his day, often portrayed by Shunsho; here he is shown, clad in vivid red, in a scene with Segawa Kikunojo II, who plays a female role.

> **Cherry Blossoms at
Asukayama** c.1778
Kiyonaga (1752-1815)

ASUKAYAMA was a beauty spot
just outside Edo (Tokyo), and
when the cherry trees came
into blossom at the end of
March, city-dwellers liked to
go there to celebrate the
coming of spring. Torii
Kiyonaga was apprenticed to
the Torii family of theatre
painters and was adopted into
the family, but his greatest
achievements were *ukiyo-e*
prints in which he set a long-
lived new fashion, replacing
the fragile beauties of
Harunobu's school with more
statuesque creatures like the
sightseers shown here. The
tiny figures in the
background include a picnic
party, one of whom is a lady
wielding a telescope to view
the more distant beauties of
nature. After his
apprenticeship, Koryusai
eventually became the head
of the Torii family, and by
1790 his new responsibilities
and prestige had virtually
ended his very successful
career as a printmaker,
leaving the way open for
Utamaro (pages 16-29).

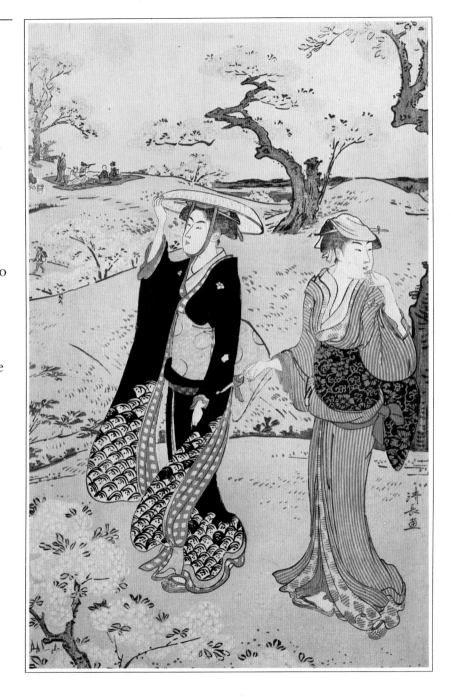

▷ **Boarding a Pleasure Boat** c.1784
Utamaro (1753-1806)

THIS IS THE FIRST unquestionable masterpiece by Kitegawa Utamaro, one of the greatest of all Japanese artists. Though very versatile, Utamaro has always been most famous for his portrayals of women, which combine grace and glamour with an unusual degree of psychological interest. *Boarding a Pleasure Boat* comes from a series named *Diversions of the Four Seasons* and is a diptych (that is, a set of two pictures). Diptychs, triptychs (sets of three) and even larger groups are frequently found in Japanese prints. In the hands of a skilful artist, each plate looked like an independent composition, yet the group could also be 'read' as a single scene. Here Utamaro's sense of design is already assured but the young women, though charming, are not yet rendered with the large confidence of his mature style. The face seen through a veil is a characteristic touch which Utamaro often employed to add piquancy or mystery to his works.

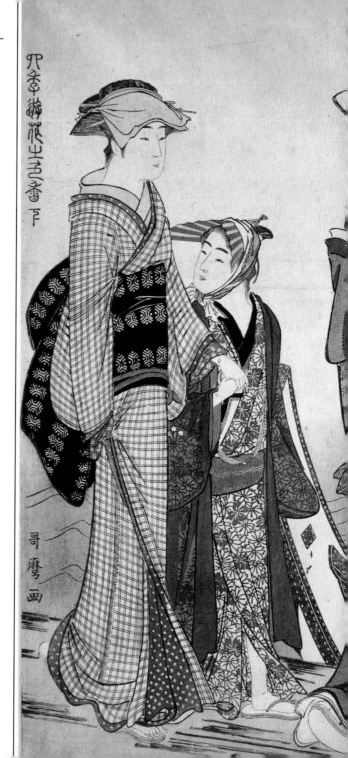

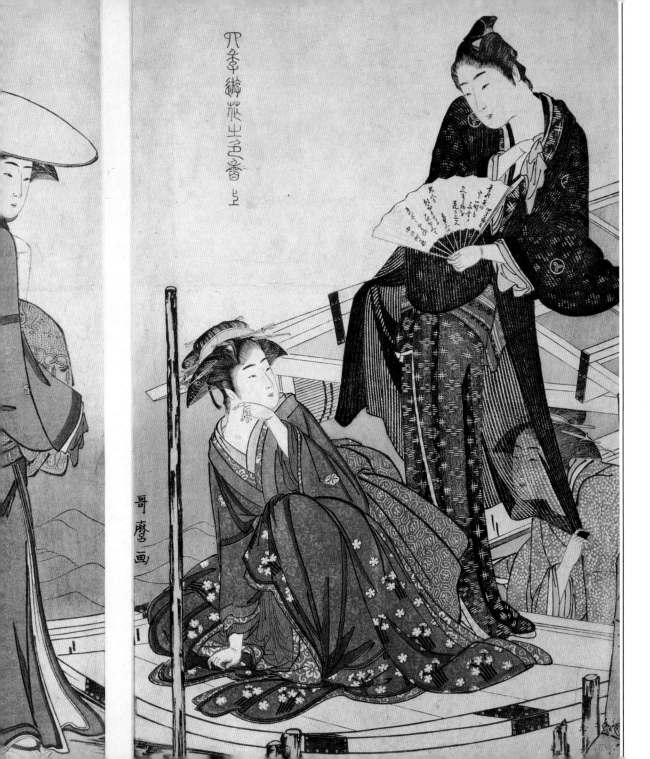

赤蜻蛉

朱楽菅江

きのふより契りてしね赤蜻蛉とんぼのおもひは
痩ひこけても

いなこ

軒端杉丸

露なからくさむらともきみまていなこのいなと
恋のくるしき

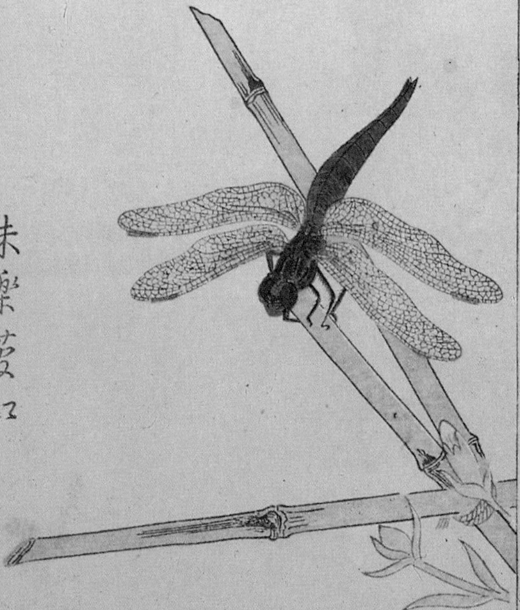

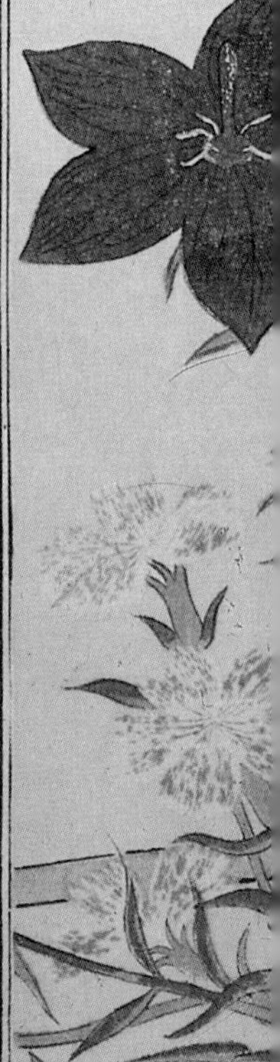

下ノ一

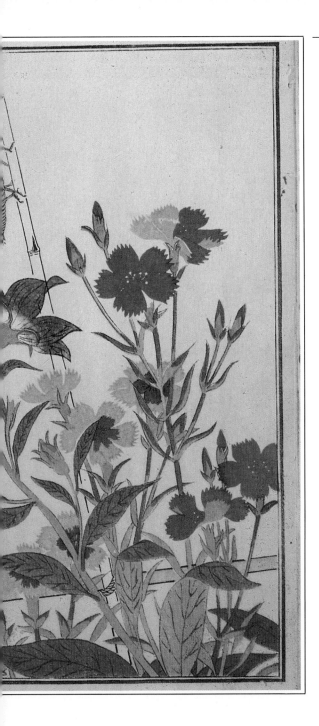

◁ **Dragonfly and Locust on a Bamboo Fence** 1788
Utamaro (1753-1806)

IN 1788-91 UTAMARO consolidated his reputation by producing three series of book illustrations . This one comes from the *Insect Book*, which was followed by two equally remarkable books about shells and birds. Though vivid and accurate, it is also highly decorative, forming a double-page design in which the characters of the poem at the left play an important part; incongruously (to western taste), the poems here and elsewhere in the book are comic and even ribald in content. Little is known of Utamaro's early life but the *Insect Book* included a postscript by his former master, Sekien, which described him as a boy in the garden of Sekien's house, capturing insects and studying them intently without doing them any harm; more provocatively, Sekien also praised Utamaro's 'painting from the heart', contrasting it favourably with the prestigious but exhausted classical tradition of painting.

▷ **Lovers** 1788
Utamaro (1753-1806)

Lovers is part of a series of
erotic prints in an album by
Utamaro, published as *The
Poem of the Pillow.* Their
explicitness and intensity are
such that westerners can still
be taken aback by them. *The
Poem of the Pillow*, ranges from
an ambiguous fantasy of
underwater sex to a rape scene
of appalling violence; and
there is also a scene involving a
Dutch man and woman (the
Dutch were the only
Europeans allowed to trade
with Japan), shown as hideous
gargoyles. The more discreetly
erotic *Lovers* is one of
Utamaro's masterpieces, with
bold forms that fill the picture,
wonderfully fluent lines and
fabrics of visibly varying
thickness; as in all his best
work, patterning and emotion
coexist in apparently effortless
fashion. The man in the scene
is often said to represent
Utamaro himself, although the
only evidence is the
resemblance between his
costume and that of the
acknowledged self-portrait
figure on page 28.

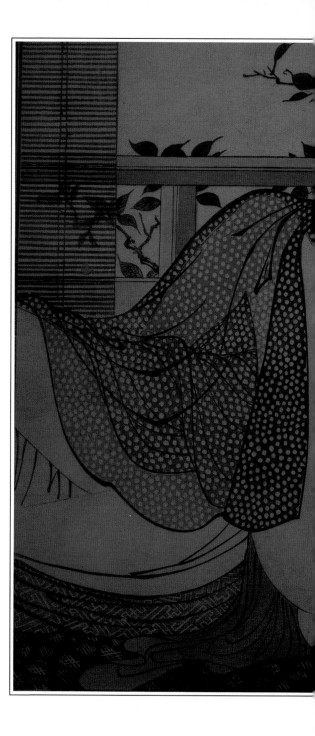

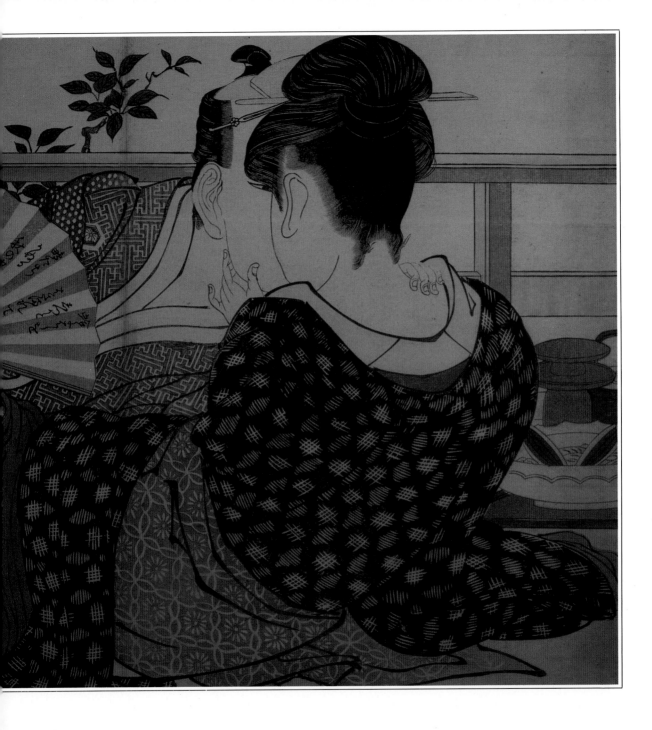

▽ **The Passionate Type** c.1792
Utamaro (1753-1806)

THE HALF-LENGTH portrait was rare in Japanese art until Utamaro introduced it in *Ten Erudite Studies of Women,* the album in which this print appeared. It was not a portrait in the sense of an image that captured the subject's likeness (something in which the Japanese had no great interest), but it did aim to convey a mood or a sense of character. The model here was a singer or teahouse beauty, probably Utamaro's favourite, O-hisa. Whether or not she convinces as 'the passionate type', she certainly has an inner life, quite distinct from (for example) that of the courtesan on page 27, dreaming of her wedding. Utamaro was clearly proud of the expressive style he had achieved in the *Ten Erudite Studies* and subsequent albums, often signing a print 'Thoughtfully drawn by Utamaro the physiognomist'.

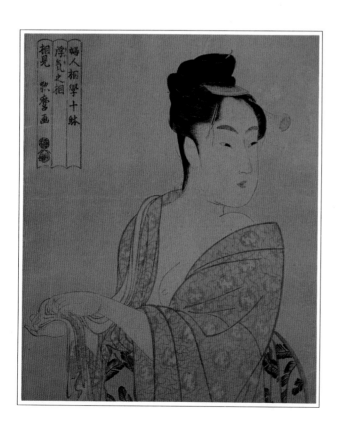

> The Hour of the Monkey
c.1795
Utamaro (1753-1806)

AT THE HEIGHT of his powers in the 1790s, Utamaro created an album with the title *The Twelve Hours of the Green Houses*. The figures portrayed are all courtesans and their maids, and the settings are the 'green houses' or brothels in the Yoshiwara (Tokyo's red-light district). The names of the hours in Japanese are based on the signs of the zodiac (the Hour of the Monkey falls between three and five o'clock in the afternoon), and Utamaro's prints show the women's activities at the various times of day. However, he does not seem to be making any particular point and it is generally believed that the scenes are simply excuses to show beautiful women in a variety of sumptuous costumes; in fact part of the appeal of *The Twelve Hours* was almost certainly as a set of fashion plates. Utamaro's women are now strikingly tall (or at least elongated) and utterly distinctive; unusually, the figure on the left is shown in profile.

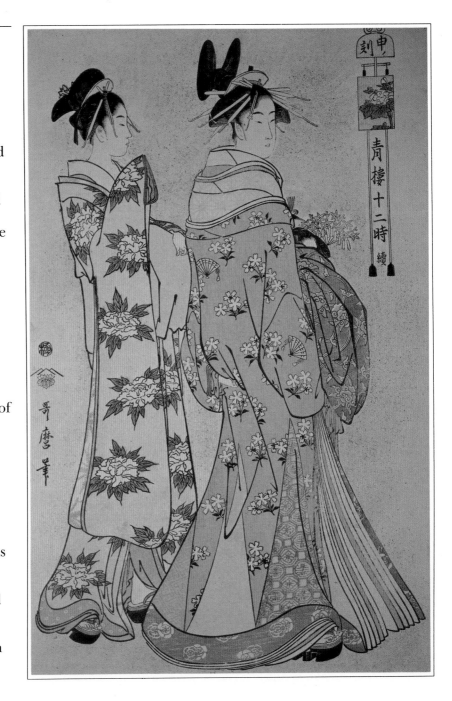

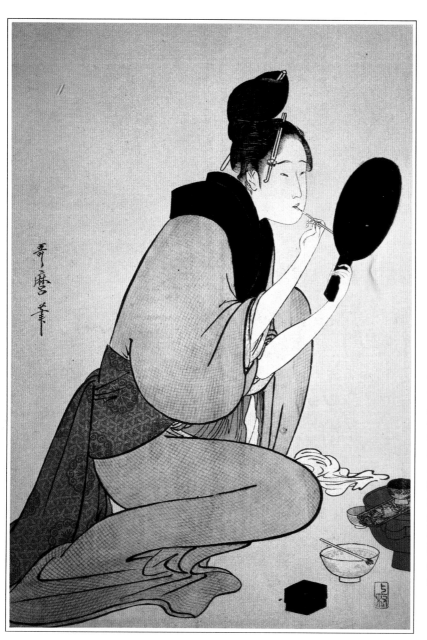

◁ **Courtesan reddening her Lips** c.1796
Utamaro (1753-1806)

IN THIS PRINT, Utamaro has taken bold stylization almost to its limit, dispensing with as much detail as possible in order to create large areas of flat colour or repeated patterns, enlivened by the fluent outlines that were one of his outstanding characteristics. Line and pattern are now so predominant that there is little sense of a body beneath the woman's kimono. Her right leg, almost touching the floor, is outlined in a sweeping fashion reminiscent of the sinuous 'whiplash line' of Art Nouveau posters in Europe and America around 1900 – a tribute to the influence of Japanese prints on western art, and also one of the reasons why Utamaro has sometimes been classed (like European artists of the 1890s) as 'decadent'. All the same, the courtesan is an enchanting creature; having lacquered her teeth, she is now colouring her lips, ready to face the duties of the day, or perhaps of the night.

▷ Three Girls in a Clothes Shop
Utamaro (1753-1806)

THE GREAT MAJORITY of Utamaro's works centre on the lives of women; but they are not always the beauties for which he was famous. He portrayed the lowest class of street-girl as well as the grand lady of pleasure and he also pictured women in more domestic roles – giving suck to infants, cleaning the house or preparing stuffs for dressmaking. *Three Girls in a Clothes Shop* is a particularly lively snapshot of everyday life with a strong sense of interaction between the girls; we can almost see them move, as one feels the fabric, her companion tests its softness on her face and the third pulls out a roll of cloth to examine it. Each is dressed in a different style, and the patterns of the costumes and fabrics set one another off in dazzling fashion. As so often in Utamaro's work, the mirror plays an important role as a symbol and also as an element in the composition.

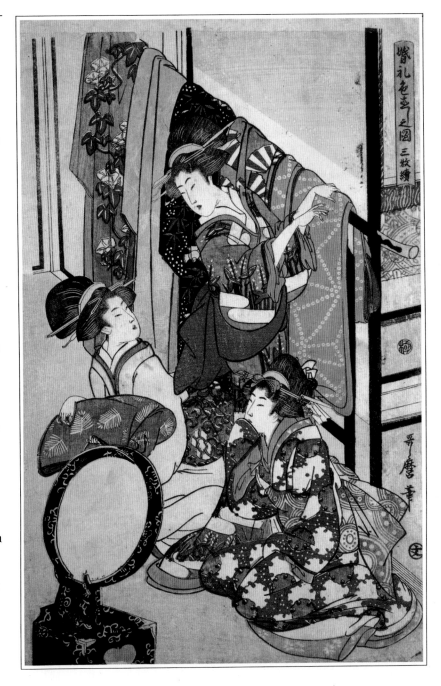

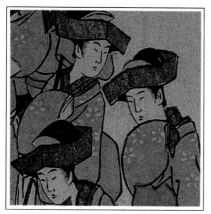

Detail

▷ **A Courtesan dreaming of her Wedding** c.1798
Utamaro (1753-1806)

ALTHOUGH THIS PRINT is complex in both design and meaning, Utamaro has laid it out with great clarity. The courtesan has put her book aside, but its contents may be responsible for the reverie in which she imagines the solemn proceedings on her wedding day. The pathos of the scene lies in the fact that the wedding will never happen, since the woman's profession has put an honourable marriage out of the question. The scene in the right-hand corner drives home the point, showing an episode from a classic tale in which the Chinese scholar Rosei sleeps on a magic pillow and dreams of marvellous, impossible things. This kind of pictorial analogy, associating the popular art of the printmakers with the hallowed classics, could be interpreted as a nose-thumbing joke or as an assertion of artistic equality, depending upon the outlook of the viewer.

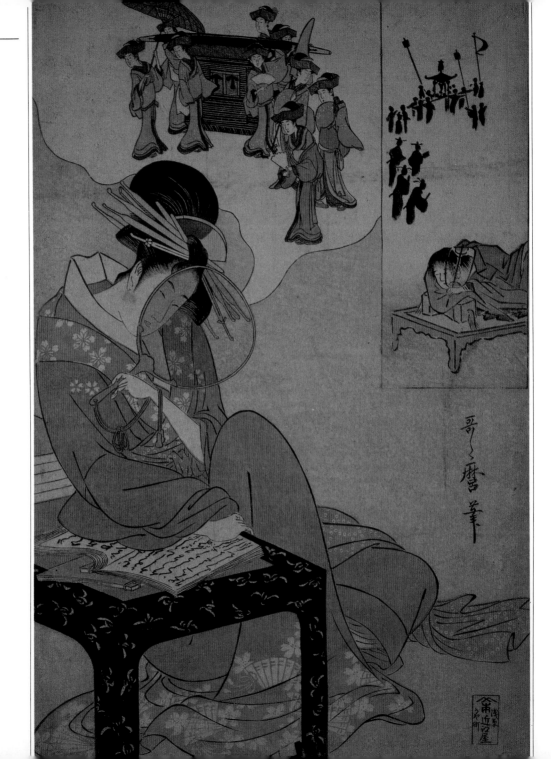

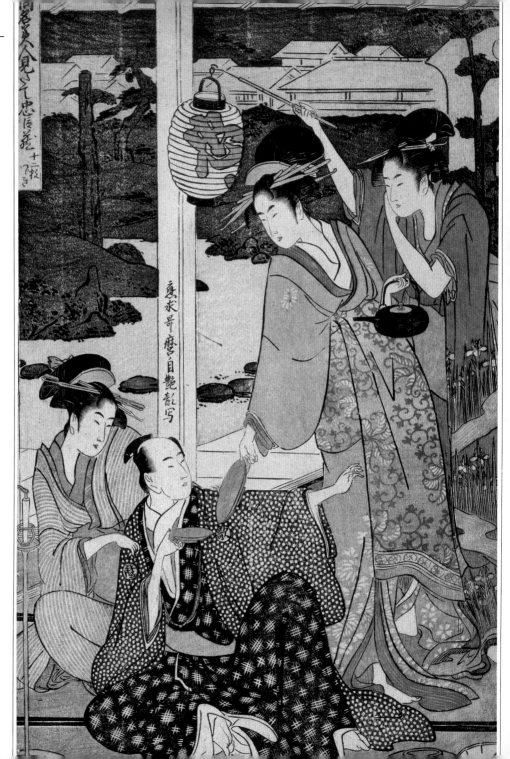

◁ **A Drinking Party in the Yoshiwara** c.1798
Utamaro (1753-1806)

UTAMARO AND HIS fellow print artists worked for a popular audience, taking their subjects and tone from the 'floating world' of city life. Their attitude towards tradition and the classics had a strong streak of irreverence, reflecting this urban outlook and, almost certainly, their own resentment at being regarded as producers of ephemera. *A Drinking Party in the Yoshiwara* comes from a series of prints parodying a celebrated tale, *The Forty-Seven Ronin*, by interpreting its heroic episodes as trivial domestic squalls. In this elegant group, the joke is taken a stage further, since the man is presented as a self-portrait of Utamaro, at ease in the Yoshiwara, the red-light district of Edo (Tokyo). An ironic-sounding caption tells us that 'To meet the general demand, Utamaro here displays his gracious portrait', though we have no means of knowing whether it actually resembled him.

Party on a Riverboat
Eishi (1756-1829)

▷ *Overleaf pages 30-31*

CHOBUNSAI EISHI seems to have been especially fond of group scenes set on boats and rafts; often, as here, the work takes the form of a number of linked plates which enabled him to show the full length of the craft. *Party on a Riverboat* might almost be seen as a follow-up to Utamaro's *Boarding a Pleasure Boat* (pages 16-17), if it were not for the graceful but remote air of the passengers which distinguishes all the women portrayed by Eishi. This has often been attributed to his unusual background: he was the scion of a wealthy, well-born family and he had enjoyed an official career and a classical training in art before turning to the gamier world of *ukiyo-e* printmaking. Having absorbed the influence of Kiyonaga and Utamaro, Eishi reached his peak in the 1790s before giving up printmaking for painting in about 1800, although he continued to work in the popular *ukiyo-e* style.

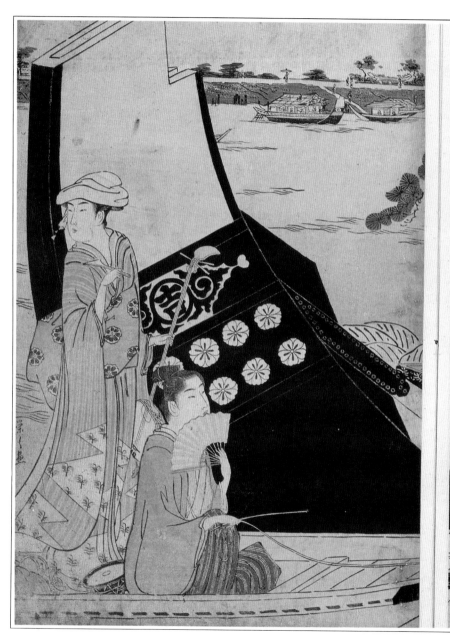
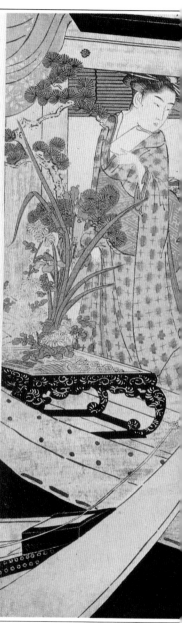

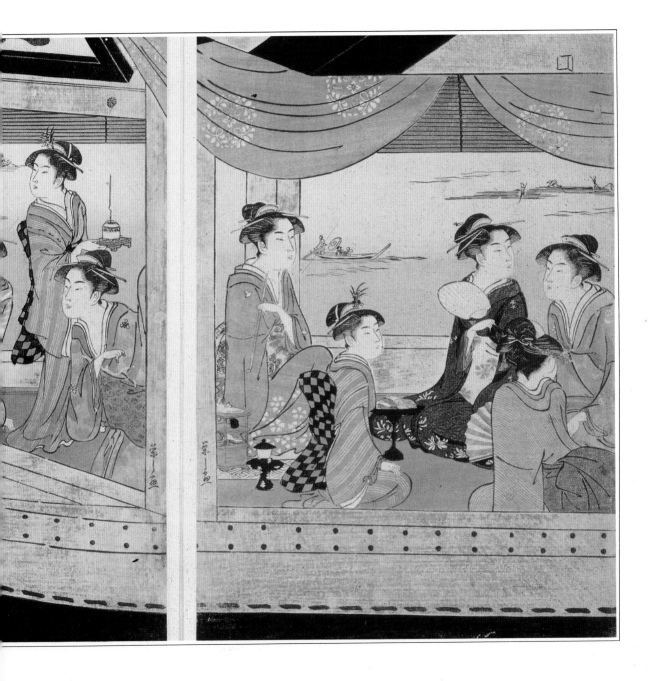

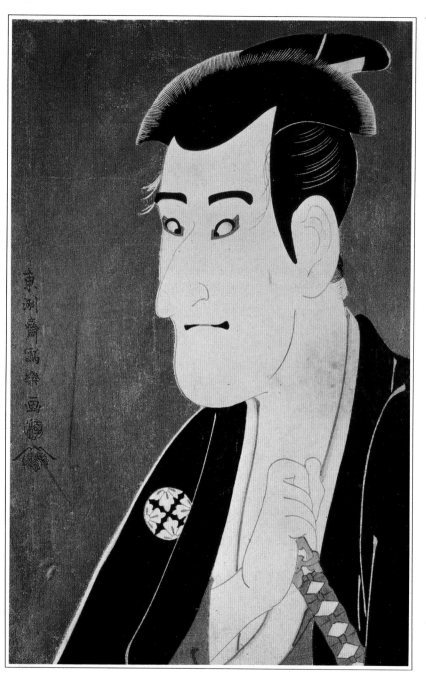

◁ **The Actor Komazo II** 1794
Sharaku (active 1794-95)

ALMOST NOTHING is known of
Toshusai Sharaku, although
his great gifts have encouraged
scholars to explore every
avenue of research: he
published about 140 superb
actor prints in the space of a
few months in 1794-95, and
then vanished as suddenly as
he had appeared. One
possibility is that he simply
changed his name: Japanese
artists frequently did so, for
example when succeeding to
the leadership of an artistic
family, or as a way of
proclaiming their allegiance to
a new style. But no convincing
identification has been made
with any contemporary artist,
and it seems more likely that
he died or even retired. There
is some evidence to suggest
that Sharaku's work failed to
sell, and since printmaking
was a business, he may have
been forced out. If so, it is all
the more ironic that he should
now be hailed as a major
innovator who portrayed his
subjects with extraordinary
realism and psychological
insight.

▷ Two Girls on New Year's Day
Eisho (active 1790s)

THIS IS AN EXAMPLE of the relatively rare pillar print, made to decorate the wooden uprights in Japanese houses, or for use as scrolls. The Japanese celebrated the New Year and sent one another greetings, often in the form of prints. The items shown here, including ferns and a crayfish, were traditionally associated with New Year festivities. Eisho was the most talented pupil of Eishi (page 29), and like many Japanese artists he demonstrated his devotion by taking a name whose first character was the same as that of his master (other pupils of Eishi called themselves Eisui, Eiri, Eiga and Eiju). We do not know when Eisho was born or when he died; he was very productive for three or four years in the late 1790s, and then is not heard of again. He seems to have been almost obsessively preoccupied with feminine beauty; if less statuesque than Eishi's, his women have greater warmth and charm.

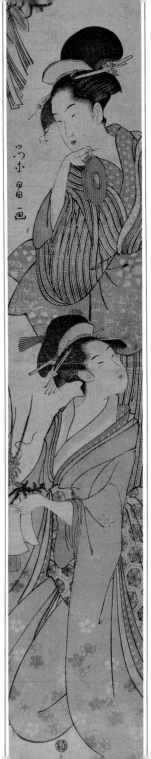

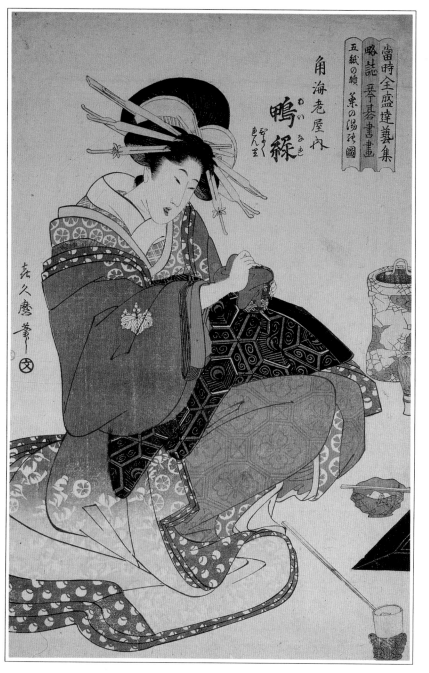

◁ **Sitting Courtesan** c.1800
Kikumaro (active 1800s)

BY THE TIME of his death in
1806, Utamaro had many
followers, including one
who, in traditional fashion,
promptly married his widow
and attempted to assume his
mantle by calling himself
Utamaro II. In the event,
only Eishi (page 29), a man
of almost Utamaro's own age,
proved able to employ the
master's style with any
consistant success. But other
disciples did have their
moments, as this study by
Kikumaro demonstrates: if
the portrayal of the woman is
not particularly inspired, the
interplay of colours and
patterns in the fabrics of her
costume is simply spell-
binding. Like other followers
of Utamaro, Kikumaro
proclaimed his allegiance by
incorporating a character from
the master's name (-maro) in
his own.

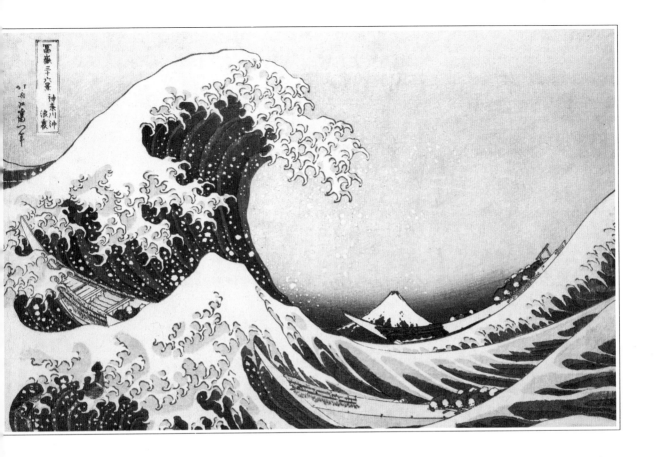

△ Beneath the Wave off Kanagawa c.1830
Hokusai (1760-1849)

IN THE WEST, this is by far the most famous Japanese print, just as its creator, Katsushika Hokusai, is the best-known Japanese artist. Often simply called *The Wave*, it belongs to a series of *Thirty-Six Views of Mount Fuji;* and the mountain does play a significant role in the composition, despite the tremendous goings-on in the foreground; Hokusai's occasional use of western-style perspective enabled him to create a sense of drama that was unusual in a scene of this kind. The tentacles of the great wave are apparently about to grasp and smother the little cargo boats, which are so dwarfed by natural forces that it is easy to overlook their presence. *The Wave* had a tremendous impact on artists – especially French artists – in the later 19th century, greatly influencing major figures such as Degas and Toulouse-Lautrec.

▷ **Mount Fuji: Southerly Wind and Fine Weather** c.1830
Hokusai (1760-1849)

LIKE THE FAMOUS *Wave* (page 35), this magnificent print comes from the series *Thirty-Six Views of Mount Fuji,* which is perhaps Hokusai's most sustained artistic achievement. In this instance, the mountain is the sole subject (the work is often called *Red Fuji*), and the wonderful balance of colour areas contributes to a sense of its majestic presence; this is of a kind that makes it much easier for an outsider to understand the religious devotion to nature which is so characteristic of the Japanese. Most Japanese mountains are sacred places but the extinct volcano Mount Fuji, or Fujiyama, is the most venerated of them all and pilgrims have long made their way there to worship the rising sun. *The Thirty-Six Views,* produced when Hokusai was in his seventies, enjoyed such popularity that he added a supplementary set of ten – but, illogically, the original title continues to be used.

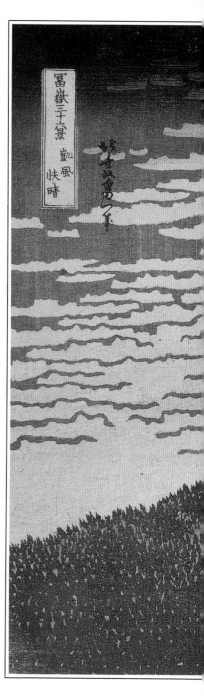

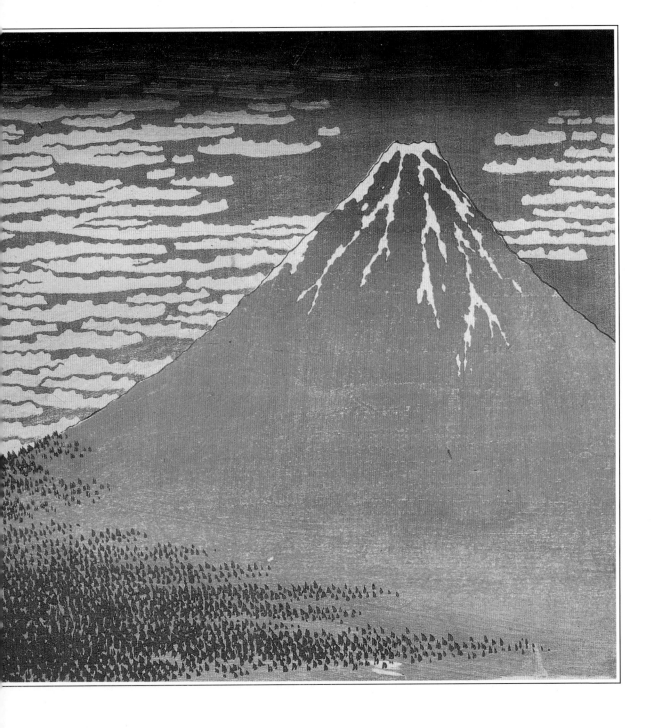

▷ **Mount Fuji from Nakahara** c.1830
Hokusai (1760-1849)

HOKUSAI'S CELEBRATED *Thirty-Six Views of Mount Fuji* shows the sacred mountain from many different directions and a variety of distances. Sometimes, as in *Southerly Wind and Fine Weather* (pages 36-37), Fuji is unmistakably the subject of the print but often the setting seems more like a pretext for views of towns and villages, tea plantations, ricefields, craftsmen at work or junks on the waters. Here, peasants and travellers are using a plank bridge over a stream at Nakahara. Although man is the principal beast of burden in the picture there is no reason to suppose that Hokusai intended to make a satirical or political statement, although, as so often in his work, the people display an almost clownish good humour. A second look at the print is likely to modify the view that the inclusion of Mount Fuji is a formality: its calm, snow-covered presence amounts to a disquieting comment on the transient busyness of the human actors.

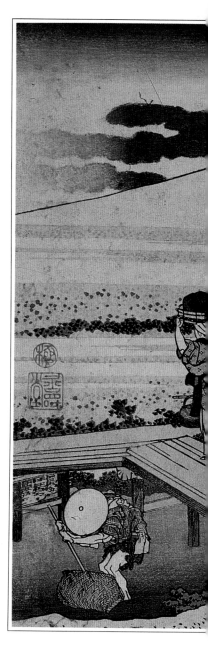

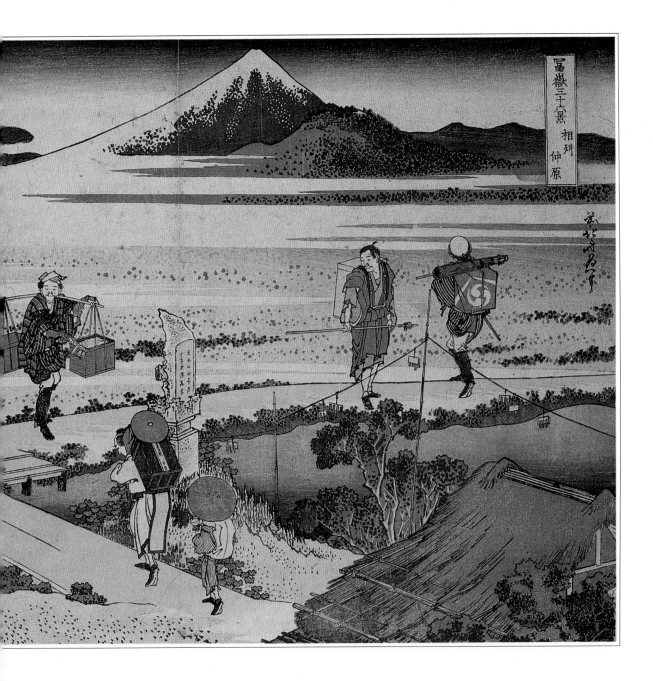

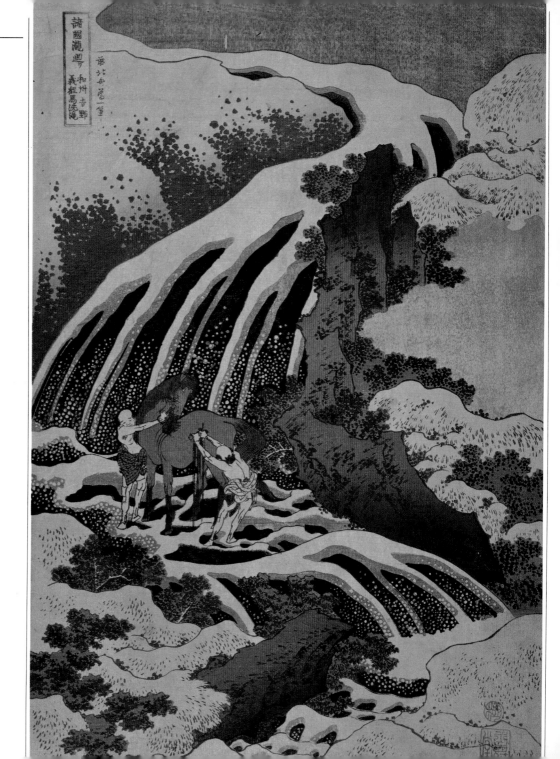

◁ **The Waterfall of Yoshino** c.1831-32
Hokusai (1760-1849)

MORE THAN ANY OTHER Japanese artist, Hokusai established the landscape print as a popular genre, on a par with courtesan and theatre scenes. He was also the greatest master of the landscape, rivalled only by his younger contemporary, Hiroshige (pages 56-65). By the 1830s the market for prints had widened, bringing in a large working-class clientele with a marked taste for souvenirs of travel or views of places which they could at least visit in imagination. The tirelessly creative Hokusai met the demand with sets of prints like the *Famous Bridges* and the *Journey to the Waterfalls of All the Provinces,* to which this view belongs. Stunningly bold in colour and design, it is hardly a literal transcription of the appearance of the falls. On the face of it, the travellers are rather prosaically taking advantage of the running water to wash down their horse; but many of Hokusai's customers would have caught the coded reference to the 11th century hero Yoshitsune, who stopped at the falls for the same purpose.

Kingfisher with Pinks and Iris c.1832
Hokusai (1760-1849)

▷ *Overleaf page 42*

HOKUSAI'S STUDIES of birds, flowers and fish are among his most expressive and beautifully composed works; over the years he made prints and paintings of such diverse subjects as domestic fowl, cranes, carp, turtles and frogs. *Kingfisher with Pinks and Iris* comes from a set of ten prints, each associating a species of bird with a particular flower and each with a Chinese poem or haiku (Japanese verse-form) added to intensify the effect. The bold colouring and general style show the influence of Chinese painting of the Ming period, which Hokusai had studied carefully in the early 1800s. The kingfisher, a darting, diving bird, is appropriately displayed in action, offsetting the large, still flowers. The blue blossoms are a type of iris that at that time were found only in Japan.

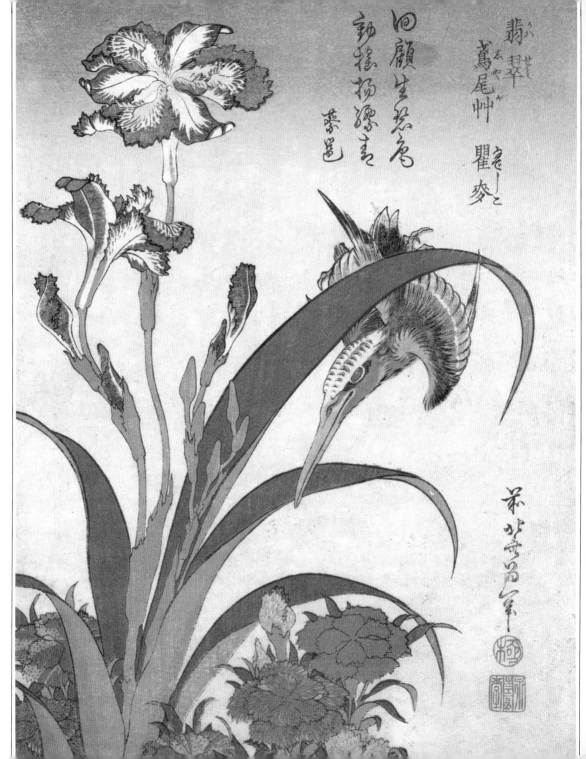

▷ **Manga**
Hokusai (1760-1849)

HOKUSAI HAS ALWAYS been more highly rated in the West than in Japan, where some connoisseurs are critical of his borrowings from non-native traditions. Equally, these may have made it easier for westerners to relate to Hokusai's works. The artist's life and personality also corresponded to the western notion of the eccentric, wayward creator. Hokusai violated the code of loyalty by studying simultaneously under two masters of different schools; he was compulsive and restless, using over thirty pen-names and he seems to have alternated between pride and humility in manic fashion. The *Manga*, or 'Random Sketches', were an expression of pride – woodblock-printed books of far-from-random drawings, intended to provide models for amateur artists. Published in fifteen volumes from 1815 onwards, they are as varied as Hokusai's paintings and colour prints, comprising an astonishingly complete record of nature and society in Japan.

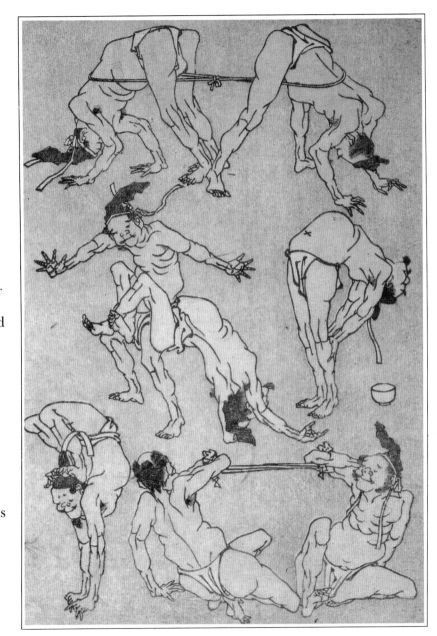

▷ **Bando Mitsugoro and Segawa Rosaburo** c.1802
Toyokuni (1769-1825)

IN WORLDLY TERMS, Utagawa Toyokuni may well have been the most successful of all Japanese print artists. The son of a woodcarver, he became the pupil of Utagawa Toyoharu, took over his master's surname, and won such fame that the 'Utagawa school' – Toyokuni and his successors – dominated the middle decades of the 19th century; Kunisada (pages 49-53) and Kuniyoshi (pages 69-75) were among his dozens of pupils. Descriptions of Toyokuni portray an artist earning an exceptionally large income, swamped with commissions and frantic in his attempts to meet deadlines, but nevertheless much given to wine, women, song and dance. His posthumous reputation suffered because of his overproduction but his mastery of the actor print remains unquestioned. Here a tense moment from a Kabuki play is sensitively rendered; although the design of the print is finely judged and the fabric patterns are exquisite, neither is allowed to interfere with the emotional impact of the performance.

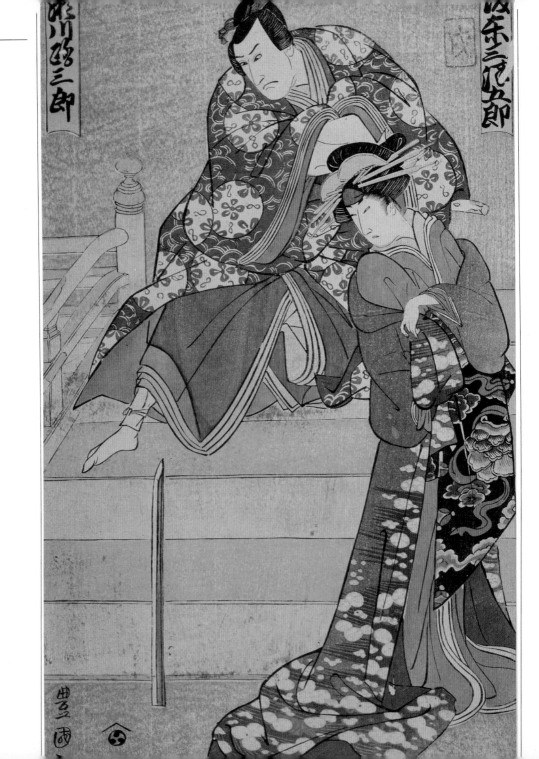

▷ **Improving Weather at
Enoshima** Early 1830s
Toyokuni II (1802-c.1835)

THIS ARTIST WAS the pupil and
son-in-law of Toyokuni (page
44), and after the master's
death assumed his name. In
itself this was a perfectly
normal and proper step,
probably approved in advance
by Toyokuni; but older and
better-established artists
(notably Kunisada, pages 49-
53) disputed Toyokuni II's
right to the succession. The
criticisms of Toyokuni II were
evidently damaging, causing
him to change his name to
Toyoshige; but posterity has
restored him to his place in the
dynasty. However, Toyokuni II
is regarded as a distinctly
minor artist, except for his
landscape prints – a single set
of *Eight Famous Views* which
suggest that, if he had lived
longer, he might have done
great things in the genre.
Enoshima, an island close to
the old capital of Kamakura,
was popular with pilgrims,
who went to worship at the
shrine of the good-luck
goddess Benten.

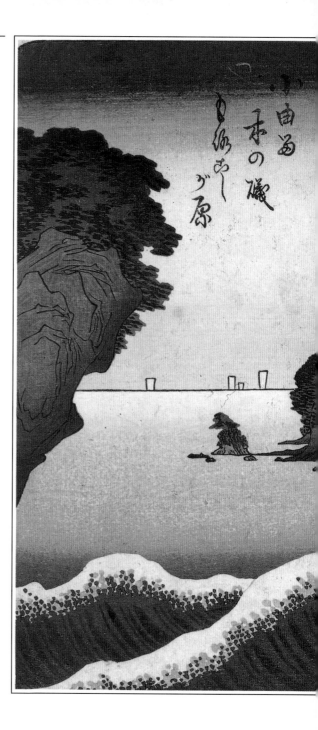

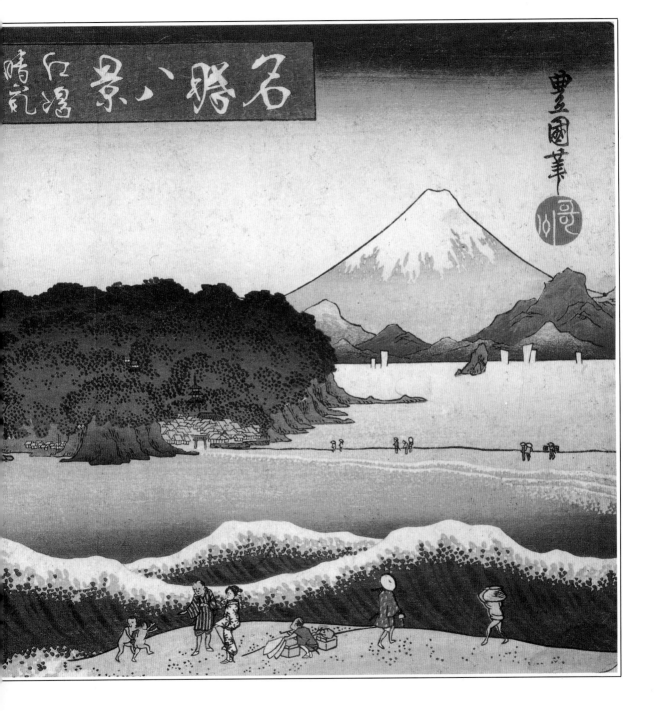

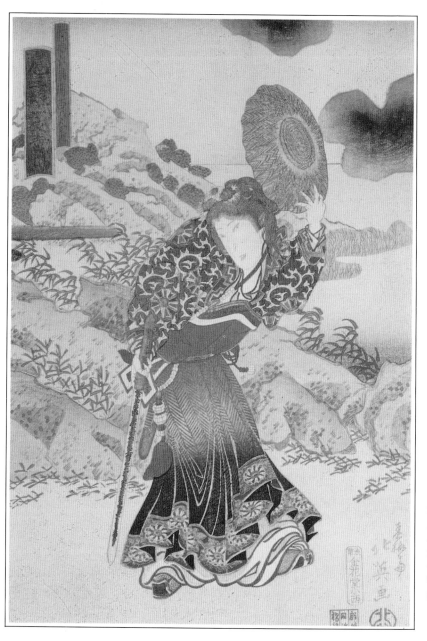

◁ **An Actor in Performance**
c.1830
Hokuei (active 1830s)

MOST OF THE GREAT Japanese print artists were either born in Edo (Tokyo) or made their careers in the city. But prints were also produced at other places, and especially Kyoto, Nagasaki and the eastern commercial centre of Osaka. Over the past few years there has been considerable interest in Osaka prints, which are predominantly of actors and scenes from the Kabuki theatre. Hokuei was a talented artist who flourished in the 1830s but disappeared from sight after 1837, when publication of prints in Osaka was suspended for some years. The name of the actor in this scene is not known, but he is playing a female role, Kosanryo Ichijosei, in a play based on a popular Chinese romance set in the 12th century. The soft tints of the print enhance the glamour that the actor is projecting, but there is a sword in his/her hand, and in the play Kosanryo Ichijosei is a distinctly strong-minded, martial figure.

▷ **The Sumo Wrestler Abumatsu Rokunosuki** 1835
Kunisada (1786-1864)

IN TRADITIONAL JAPAN sumo champions were popular heroes and portrait prints of them were sold alongside those of glamorous courtesans and actors, apparently without any sense of incongruity. Size, weight and strength were indispensable for success, and many celebrated wrestlers were reputed to have been mighty and mountainous even as children. Dexterity also played a part in achieving victory, since the object of the contest was to make the opponent step outside the ring or touch the ground with some part of his body other than the soles of his feet. When the appropriate ceremonial was completed, the actual bout generally lasted for no more than a few seconds. Kunisada's clever design emphasizes his hero's enormous bulk, which is framed so that the picture seems only just able to fit it all in.

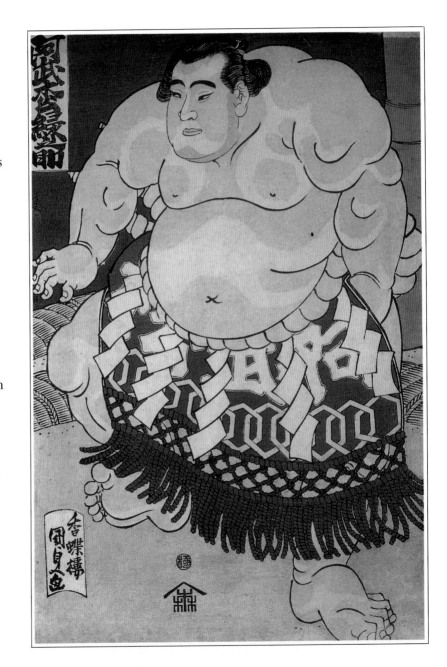

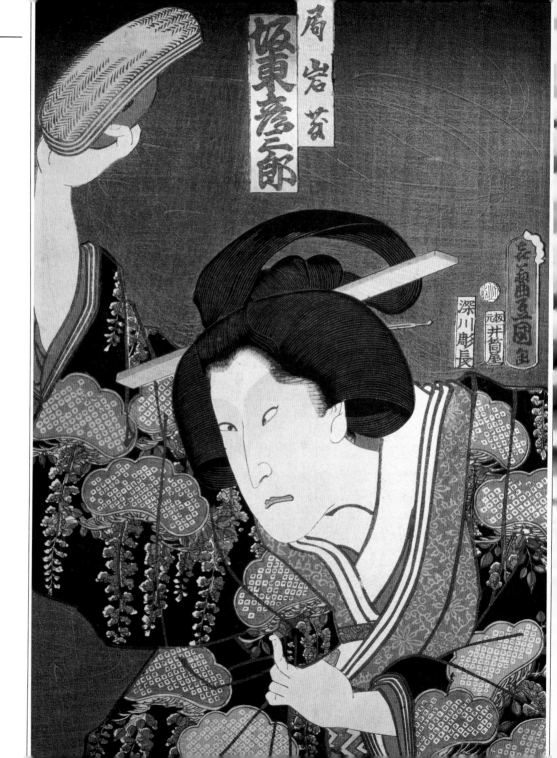

◁ **Bando Hikosaburo** c.1850 Kunisada (1786-1864)

IN THIS POWERFULLY realized portrait of an actor in a kabuki drama, Bando Hikosaburo is playing an infuriated lady in waiting who is about to beat an underling with her sandal. The crossed eyes were an accepted convention used to represent extremes of emotion. Part of the actor's skill was to intensify his physical reaction to a dramatic situation and then, at the very height of his simulated passion, to hold his pose, creating a set piece called a *mie*. Although kabuki had been originated by a female troupe in the early 17th century, fights between their admirers had proved so troublesome that the government decreed that only men could take part. The actors who specialized in female parts became stars in their own right, often setting fashions that were taken up by their women admirers. Like artists, they often took the names of famous predecessors, and such dynasties – like that of Bando Hikosoburo – might last for a century or more.

The Moon 1857 Kunisada (1786-1864)

▷ *Overleaf pages 52-53*

THIS PLEASANT GLIMPSE of traditional Japanese life is full of recognizable images: the light wooden frames of the houses, the partitions and blinds, the absence of furniture apart from mats, the lacquered containers, the lovely fans and fabrics. Through the window lies the kind of misty landscape normally associated with classic paintings rather than prints; and over it all presides the moon, for whose beauty and symbolism the Japanese had a particularly keen appreciation. By the time this print was published, Kunisada had been in the forefront of *ukiyo-e* artists for almost half a century. Apprenticed to Toyokuni at the age of fifteen, he produced his first independent book illustration in 1807 and his first actor print, the genre in which he would dominate his generation, the following year. Kunisada is believed to have been the most prolific of all printmakers, producing thousands of works of all types, from ghost stories to landscapes.

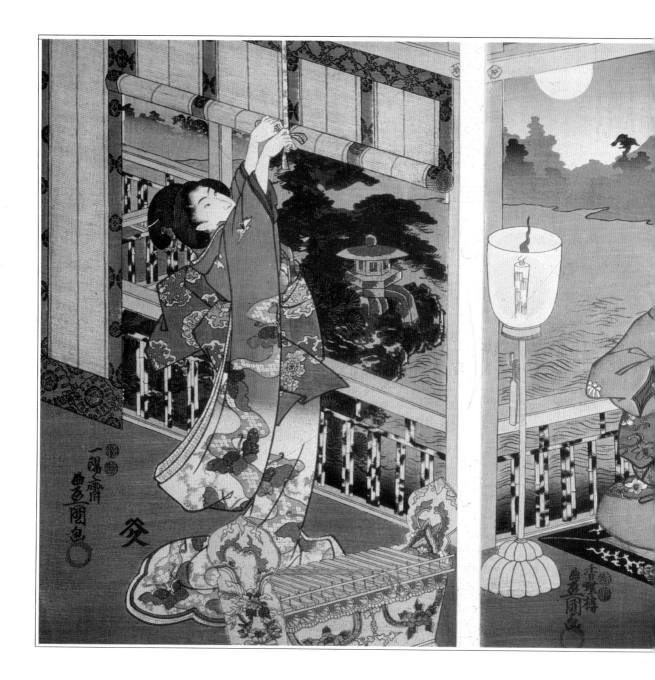

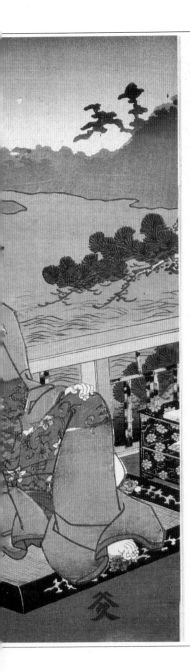
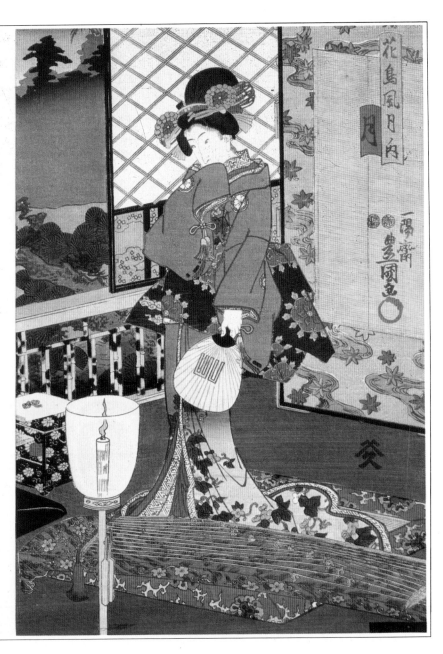

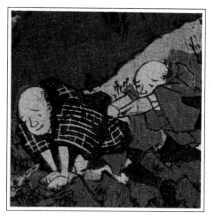

Detail

▷ **The Kegon Falls at Nikko** c.1830s
Eisen (1790-1848)

KEISA EISEN was a prolific and very popular print artist, most of whose output was devoted to courtesan subjects. However, posterity has preferred his landscapes, notably those in *The Sixty-Nine Stations of the Kiso Highway* (c.1839) by Eisen and Hiroshige. This was not a true collaboration, for Hiroshige was called in after Eisen had quarrelled with the publisher and left; but Eisen's twenty-four works in the series stand up well to comparison with those of the acknowledged master-landscapist of the Japanese print. Though he was the pupil of a very fine artist, Kikukawan Eizan (1787-1867), Eisen was also strongly influenced by Hokusai and it is interesting to compare *The Kegon Falls* with a similar subject by the older man. Eisen's version has its own bold and dramatic quality, emphasizing the height of the falls, but it is the three visitors, full of comic delight at the spectacle, who give the scene its distinctive tone.

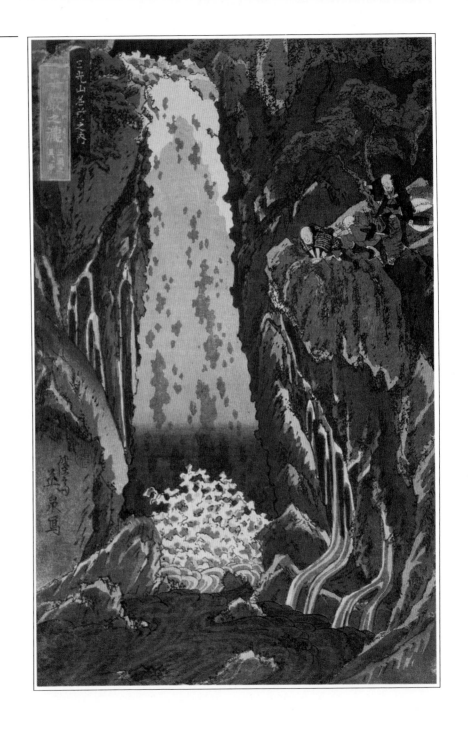

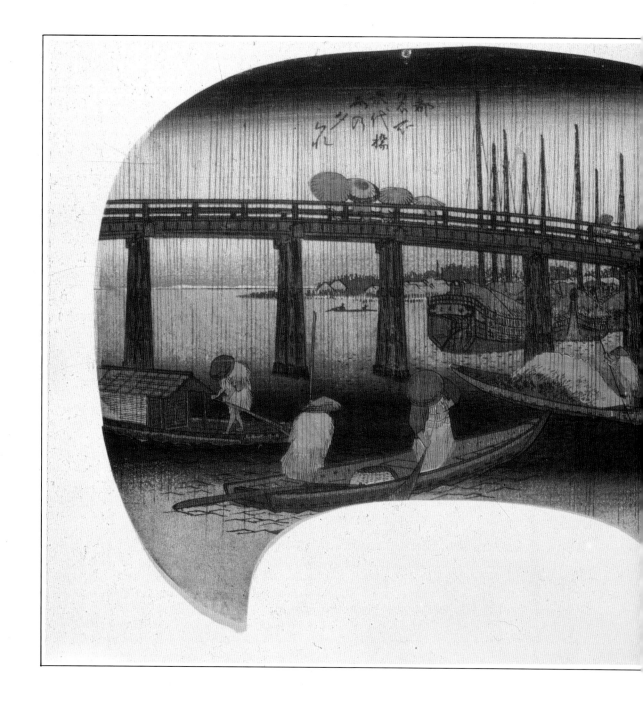

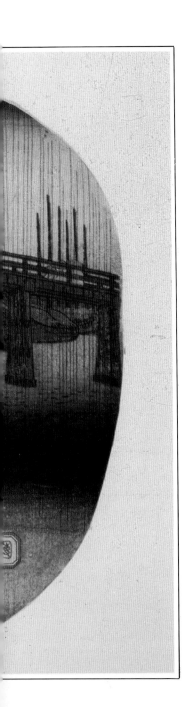

◁ **Etai Bridge in the Evening Rain** c.1835
Hiroshige (1797-1858)

THE CURIOUS SHAPE of this picture is explained by the fact that it is a fan with a scene printed on it. Fan prints are relatively rare, although the evidence suggests that they were made in large numbers; presumably they simply became worn out. The regular use of such an object, decorated with the work of a master, is an impressive example of the aesthetic attitude to everyday living, but also bears out the view that colour prints, while appreciated by the Japanese, were regarded as essentially ephemeral productions. For fairly obvious reasons, folding fan prints are even rarer than the kind shown here, with a rigid surface. The view of Etai Bridge is from one of several series by Hiroshige with the title *Famous Places of Edo*. One of his most successful effects was the heavy shower, rendered with deceptive simplicity by near-parallel lines. The impact of the rain is admirably conveyed by huddled boatmen and pedestrians bent beneath their umbrellas.

▷ **Travellers in the Snow** c.1839
Hiroshige (1797-1858)

THE POPULAR ART of the print
was dominated by city
concerns (courtesans, actors,
etc.) until landscapes and
views were established as
equally important subjects by
Hokusai and his younger
contemporary Hiroshige. Less
forceful but more lyrical than
Hokusai, Hiroshige became
the best-loved of all print
artists in his native land. Some
of his most celebrated early
works are travel series,
following the two great routes
from Edo to Kyoto via the
post-stops on the way: *The
Fifty-Three Stations of the
Tōkaido,* the coastal route, and
*The Sixty-Three Stations of the
Kiso Highway,* executed jointly
with Eisen. The Kiso Highway
was the mountainous inland
route, and *Travellers in the Snow*
shows how hostile it could be.
The travellers are hidden
beneath their hats and capes
for practical reasons but this
has also allowed Hiroshige to
make the scene a *tour de force*
of white-on-white. Here, as
elsewhere, the decorative
possibilities of the flat, round
hats are exploited to great
effect.

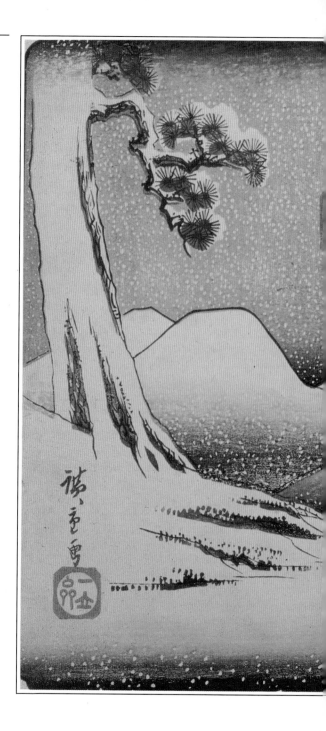

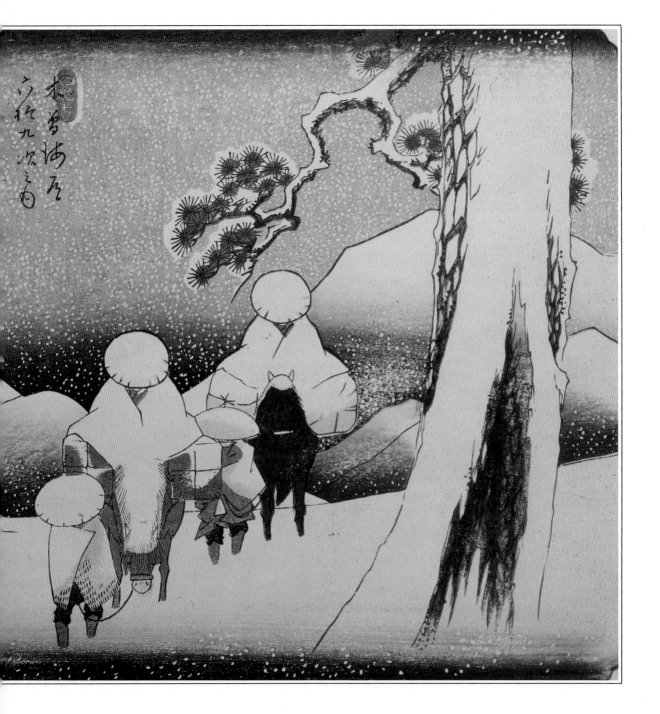

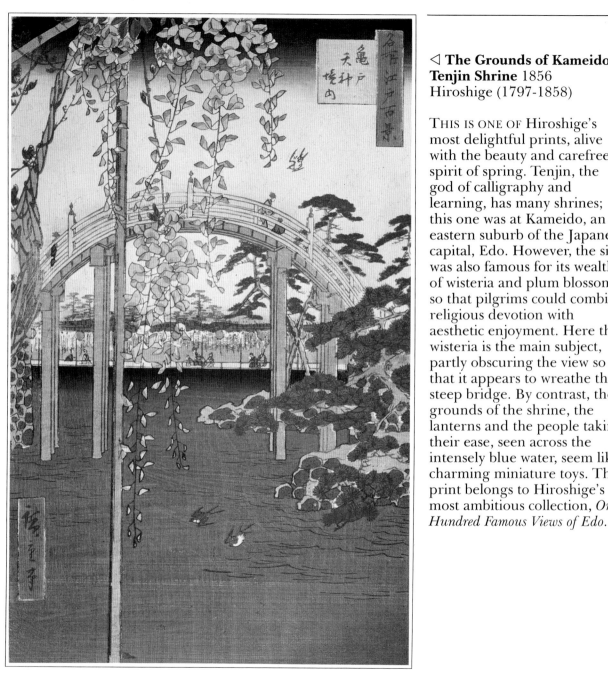

◁ **The Grounds of Kameido Tenjin Shrine** 1856
Hiroshige (1797-1858)

THIS IS ONE OF Hiroshige's most delightful prints, alive with the beauty and carefree spirit of spring. Tenjin, the god of calligraphy and learning, has many shrines; this one was at Kameido, an eastern suburb of the Japanese capital, Edo. However, the site was also famous for its wealth of wisteria and plum blossom, so that pilgrims could combine religious devotion with aesthetic enjoyment. Here the wisteria is the main subject, partly obscuring the view so that it appears to wreathe the steep bridge. By contrast, the grounds of the shrine, the lanterns and the people taking their ease, seen across the intensely blue water, seem like charming miniature toys. The print belongs to Hiroshige's most ambitious collection, *One Hundred Famous Views of Edo.*

> **View of Mitsumata** 1857
Hiroshige (1797-1858)

THIS IS A RATHER unusual
foreigner's-eye view' from out
at sea, showing the delta of the
Sumida River, with the city of
Edo (Tokyo) in the distance
and, still further away, Mount
Fuji. The foreground is
occupied by cargo boats and a
marshy island that hardly rises
above the level of the water. A
picture of this kind might be
regarded as a kind of
substitute for travel, since
Japan's rulers, the Tokugawa,
had deliberately isolated the
country from 1638,
prohibiting foreign travel and
even forbidding the return of
any Japanese who happened
to be abroad at the time. The
enormous popularity of views
and travel pictures by Hokusai
and Hiroshige suggests that
the Japanese were becoming
restless; ironically, *View of
Mitsumata* appeared at a time
when actual foreigners – the
American Commodore Perry
and his ships – had forced
Japan to renew contact with
the outside world, beginning a
new era that would disrupt the
traditional order.

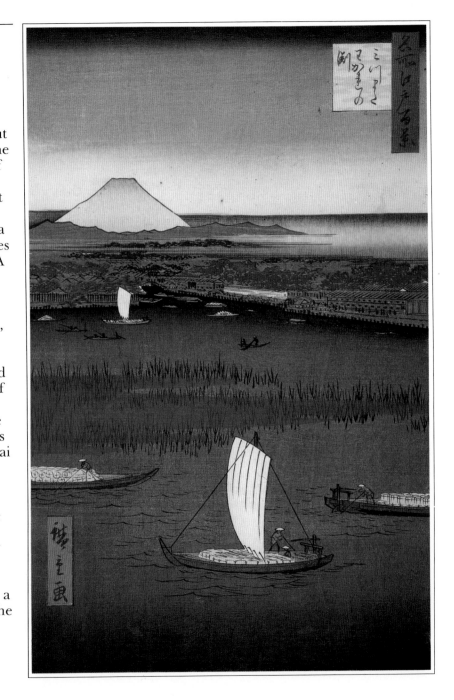

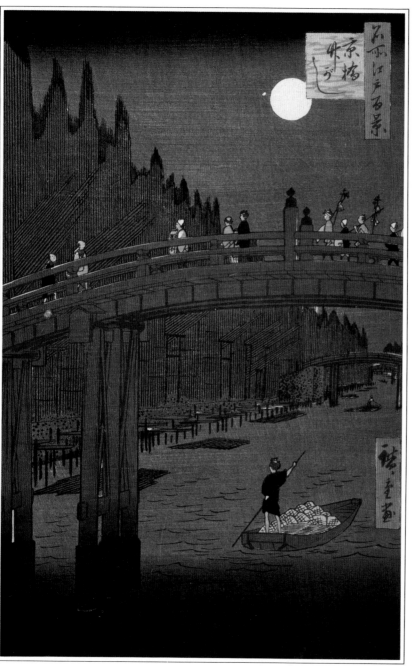

◁ **Bamboo Embankment, Kyobashi** c.1857
Hiroshige (1797-1858)

KYOBASHI IS CLOSE to the mouth of the Sumida River, which flows through Edo (Tokyo). Hiroshige has created a peaceful scene from conventional elements – the night, the moon, bridges, a heavy-laden boat and some rafts – but the looming bamboo embankment strengthens the composition, saving it from banality. The print belongs to the series *One Hundred Famous Views of Edo;* it gains by being seen as part of a set, since that reveals Hiroshige's remarkable powers of observation and the variety of sights to be seen in and around the city, from blossoms and temples to canals and cotton-goods shops. During the course of his career Hiroshige tended to move away from landscapes (in the strict sense of the word), mainly devoting himself to views of Edo; the famous one hundred was by no means his only collection. One critic has suggested that his studies of conditions on the great highways (page 59) converted him once and for all to the comforts of city life!

> **Maple Trees with Tekona Shrine and Bridge** 1857
Hiroshige (1797-1858)

HERE HIROSHIGE has used the same device as in *The Grounds of Kameido Tenjin Shrine* (page 60), viewing a distant scene through a screen of vegetation that seems to be just in front of the spectator. The shrine in *Maple Trees* is even further away, creating a cooler, more tranquil mood that is appropriate to the season; in the autumn, a citizen of Edo might well make a special trip to a local beauty spot to view the red maple leaves, having gone to other places in spring to see the wisteria or cherry blossom. Hiroshige's strangely moving juxtaposition of 'the near and the far' is quite distinctive, although it almost certainly owes something to the study of perspective in western painting, which had begun to influence artists of his generation.

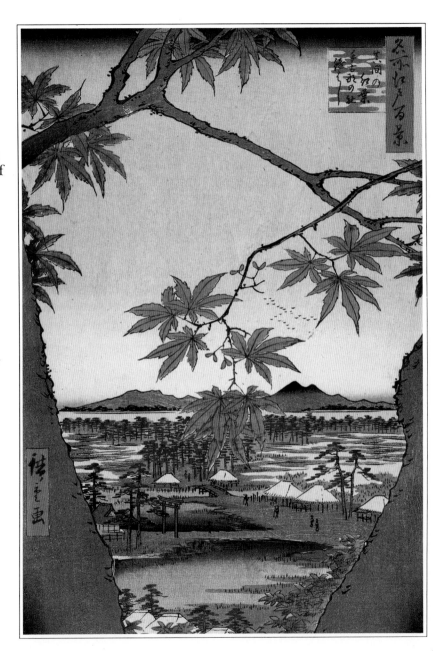

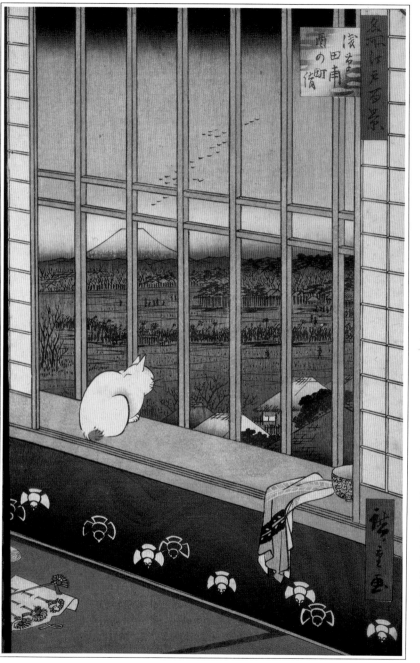

◁ **Asakusa Ricefields, Cock Festival** 1857
Hiroshige (1797-1858)

LIKE SO MANY scenes by
Hiroshige, *Asakusa Ricefields*
brings home the way in which
town and country were
intermixed in old Japan,
making it easy to leave behind
cramped and often squalid
dwellings. (This was, of course,
true of cities everywhere,
including Europe, until the
full development of industry in
the 19th century.) So the
incongruity of putting such a
print among the *Hundred
Famous Views of Edo* is apparent
rather than real. Asakusa was
(and is) a district in the heart
of Edo, famous for its
Buddhist shrine dating back to
the 7th century. Hiroshige's
view brings together interior
and exterior, cultivated fields
and untamed nature (Mount
Fuji), the domestic cat and
flights of birds, providing
much to meditate upon. The
cock was one of the creatures
in the Japanese zodiac; the
Cock Festival took place in
mid-November but the
merrymaking associated with
it is only hinted at here.

> **Fireworks at Ryogoku** 1858
Hiroshige (1797-1858)

HIROSHIGE HAS COMPOSED this
night scene with extraordinary
skill, balancing the elements
and picking out all the salient
details without violating our
sense of realities. It is one of
his last works, created in the
year of the great cholera
epidemic that carried him off,
along with many other
inhabitants of Edo; however,
he evidently had more than
enough time to complete the
Hundred Famous Views of the
city (of which this is one), since
the final total was actually 119!
Firework displays were
extremely popular summer
entertainments, held over
water to reduce the risk of
starting a fire in a city of
wooden buildings. The big
bridge at Ryogoku is shown
crowded with onlookers, while
gaily lamplit boats cluster
below it. The dying fall of the
spent rocket is balanced by the
multiple firecracker
explosions. The signature and
seals of Japanese prints are
always skilfully integrated into
the designs, but never more so
than here, where they help to
brighten the night sky.

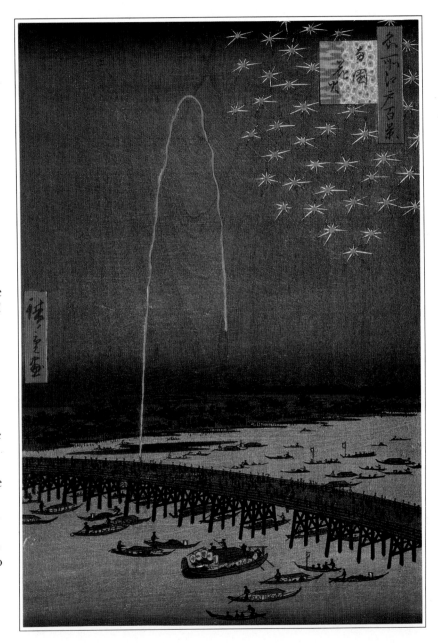

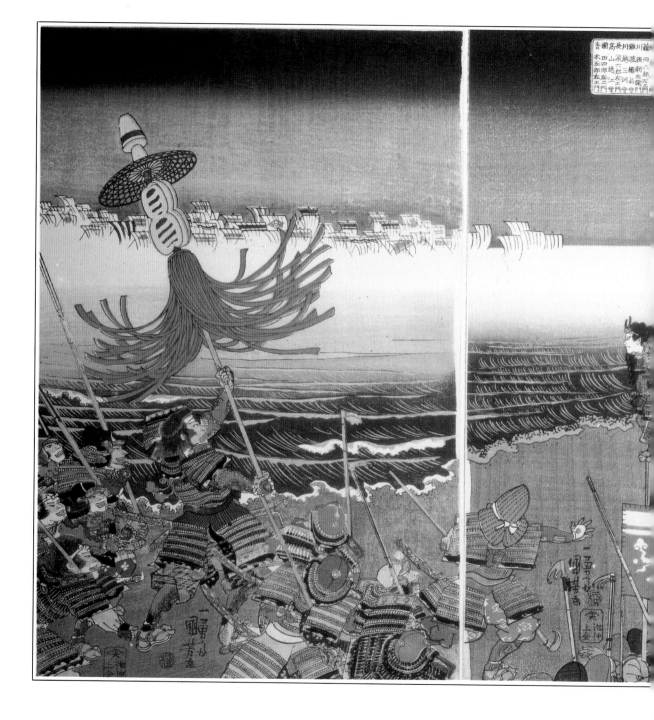

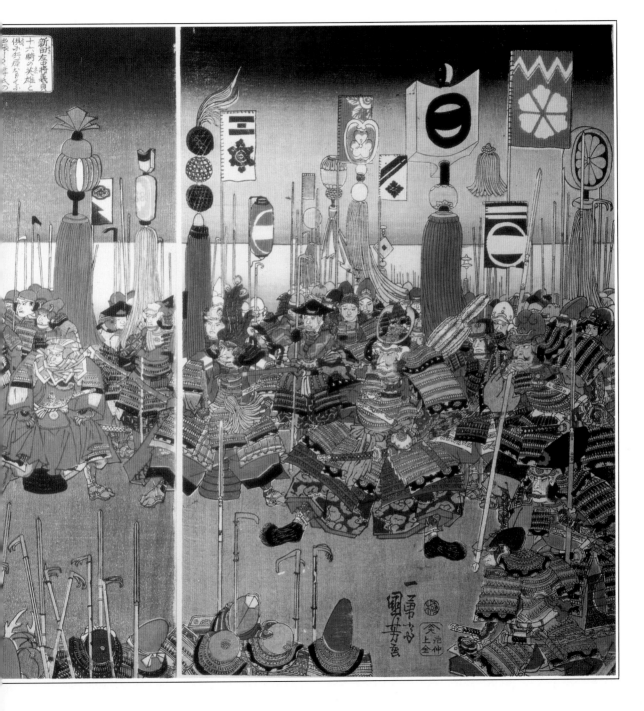

The Ashikaga Fleet sailing to attack Nitta c.1840 Kuniyoshi (1798-1861)

◁ *Previous pages 66-67*

LIKE HIS OLDER contemporary Kunisada (pages 49-53), Utagawa Kuniyoshi was the pupil of Toyokuni (page 44). But although he followed his master's example for a time by making actor prints, he found his own style, and his distinctive subject matter, in the late 1820s. Kuniyoshi drew on Japan's blood-soaked medieval history, which had rarely been exploited by printmakers, to create a new kind of bold, brash, colourful art; and the public, after three hundred years of peace, responded enthusiastically to his pictures of epic struggles and desperate last stands. In the triptych shown here, the rebel Ashikaga clan has gathered a huge fleet and is sailing to attack the emperor's army, led by the redoubtable Nitta Yoshisada. Partly hidden by the mist, the fleet is an ominous sight. No Japanese needed to be told the outcome: at the battle of the Minatogawa, which took place on 4 July 1336, the emperor's army was annihilated and the 230-year dominance of the Ashikaga began.

▷ The Flight of Tokiwa-gozen c.1842 Kuniyoshi (1798-1861)

TOKIWA-GOZEN was the beautiful mistress of Minamoto no Yoshitomo, a 12th century magnate who was defeated and killed in one of the wars between the Minamoto and Taira clans. Kuniyoshi's print pictures Tokiwa-gozen's subsequent flight through the snow. Her struggle to make her way against the wind is conveyed with superb skill but at first the viewer may not notice the two faces visible through an opening in her cloak and the two small pairs of feet above the snow. Tokiwa-gozen is shielding two of her children by Yoshimoto and in fact also carries a baby at her breast. The three herons in flight are no doubt their symbolic counterparts. Tokiwa-gozen succeeded in reaching safety but was forced to return to the court and, in order to save her sons, became the mistress of the Taira leader, Kiyomori. However, poetic justice was done, for her sons Yoshitsune and Yorimoto lived to bring about the utter destruction of the Taira.

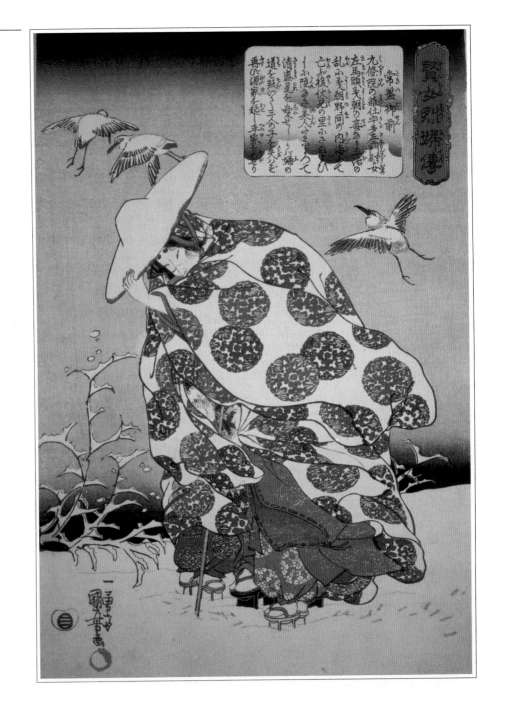

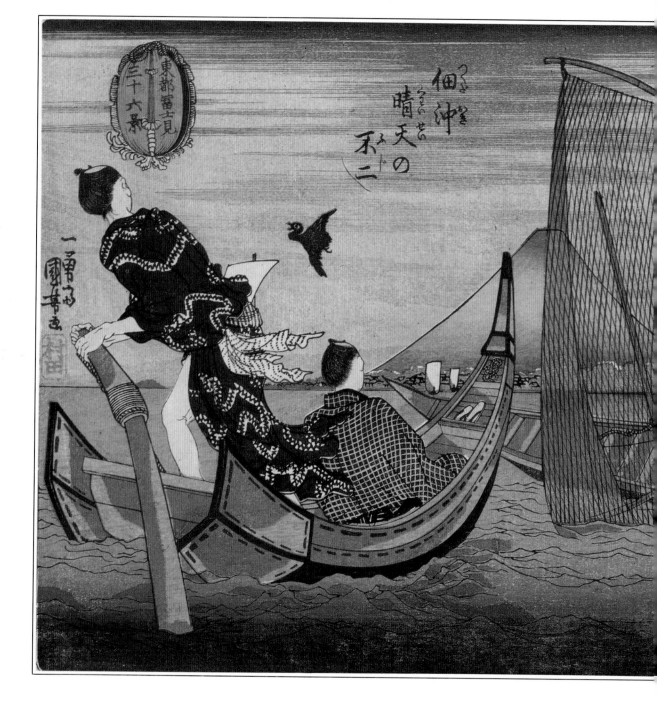

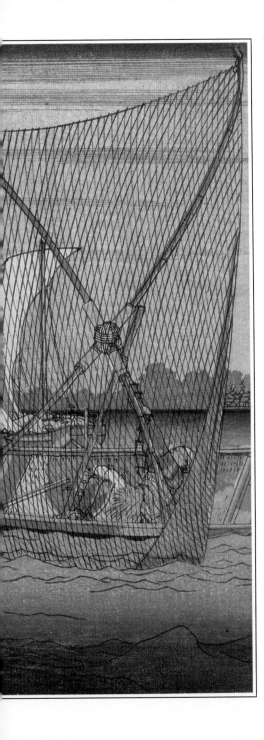

◁ **Mount Fuji seen from Edo Bay** c.1843
Kuniyoshi (1798-1861)

FOR A LONG TIME, printmaking was supposed to have been in terminal decline from the early 19th century, with Hokusai and Hiroshige as the last, brilliant representatives of a dying art. Kuniyoshi's work was ignored, despite its popularity during his lifetime, presumably because its distinctive brand of dynamism and drama was considered 'un-Japanese' and his warrior prints did not fit in with the established image of *ukiyo-e*. In recent years all that has changed, and books and exhibitions have made Kuniyoshi widely known as well as accepted by critics as one of the great Japanese masters. The print reproduced here comes from the series *Thirty-Six Views of Mount Fuji seen from Edo*. The title deliberately echoes that of Hokusai's views and can only be read as a challenge to the older master. Kuniyoshi has perhaps not equalled Hokusai's achievement as a landscapist but the large foreground figures and sense of vigour did bring something new to the genre.

▷ The Death of Tomomori
c.1844
Kuniyoshi (1798-1861)

KUNIYOSHI WAS at his most prolific and creative during the 1840s. Already much in demand, his warrior prints were further favoured by the removal of competition when a government decree of 1842 banned the two mainstays of popular art, courtesan and actor prints. Among the high heroic moments that most appealed to the Japanese were hopeless last stands, gallantly conducted to the end, and self-destruction in the face of impossible odds: seppuku, or ritual disembowelment, if there was time; if not, a spectacular gesture that might be remembered for centuries. Such was the end of the Taira commander Shinchunagon Tomomori at the battle of Dan-no-ura (1185). Seeing that all was lost, and close to death from his wounds, he wound a huge anchor round his body and flung himself into the sea. Tomomori appears in the central panel of the triptych; the two side panels show the defiant figures of his loyal retainer and his mistress.

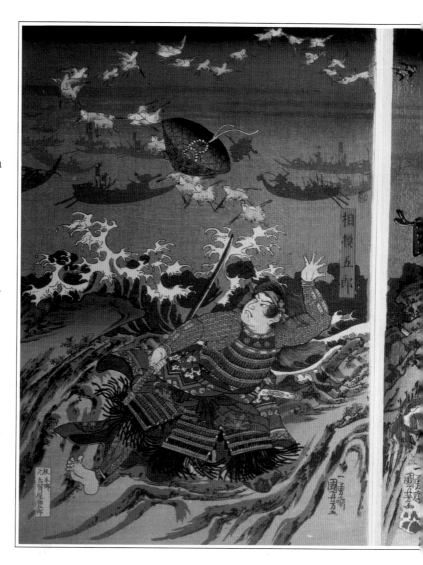

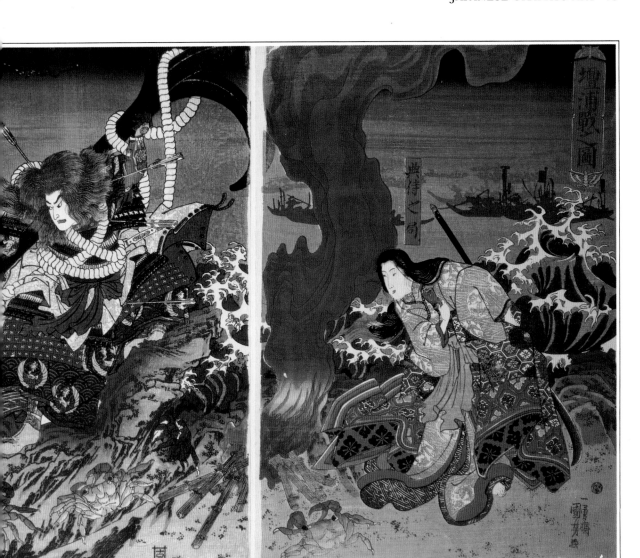

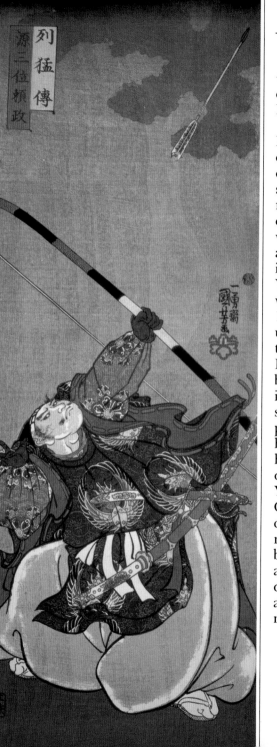

◁ **Yorimasa shooting at Nuye**
c.1845
Kuniyoshi (1798-1861)

KUNIYOSHI'S GENIUS for conveying action is at its most effective in this straightforward portrayal of resolution and effort. It is also one of many examples of the way in which Japanese history and legend became intertwined. Minamoto no Yorimasa was a real person who committed seppuku in 1180 after taking part in an unsuccessful rebellion against the Taira shogun Fujimori. But Kuniyoshi's work harks back to 1153, when Yorimasa is said to have been summoned to the imperial palace after the emperor heard strange noises above his head. Noticing a black cloud descend on the palace roof, Yorimasa loosed an arrow at it. Out of the cloud fell a monster called the Nuye, with a monkey's head, a badger's body, a tiger's claws and legs, and a snake tail! Kuniyoshi has discreetly shown us the arrow and the cloud, leaving the monster to our imaginations.

> **Mongaku Shonin under the Waterfall** c.1852
Kuniyoshi (1798-1861)

THIS IS THE bottom panel of a triptych which is, unusually, arranged vertically, emphasizing the long columns of falling water. All that the viewer really needs to know is that the monk Mongaku Shonin is enduring the icy waters as an act of penitence, watched over by an acolyte of a Buddhist deity, Fudo, who dominates the top panel of the triptych. However, the monk's crime is of interest as the climax of a typically Japanese tale of virtue, self-sacrifice and horror. A young man named Morito pursued his married cousin so relentlessly that she pretended to give in – on condition that he murdered her husband. Morito crept into the husband's bedroom and cut off his head, only to find that the faithful wife had substituted herself for him. The grieving husband contemptuously refused to kill the culprit and Morito shaved his head and became the monk Mongaku Shonin.

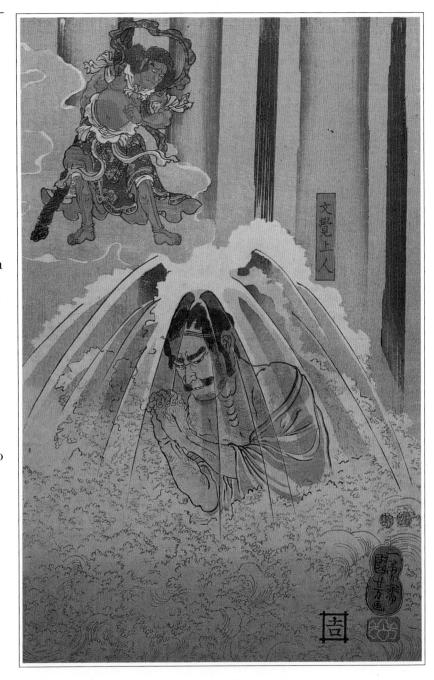

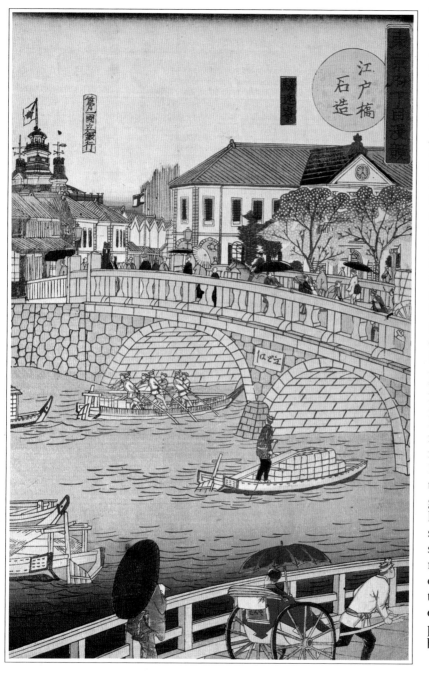

◁ The Stone Bridge at Edobashi
Hiroshige III (1841-94)

THE 'DYNASTIC' ELEMENT in Japanese art is particularly evident in the events following the death of the great Hiroshige in 1858. Hiroshige's adopted son married the artist's daughter, Otatsu, and assumed the name Hiroshige II. But when the marriage was dissolved (about 1865) Hiroshige II changed his name again, while another former pupil promptly married Otatsu and began to call himself Hiroshige II; historians have avoided possible confusion by re-labelling him Hiroshige III. Despite his prestigious name, Hiroshige III was a man of the new Meiji era, when Japan was rapidly becoming westernized. In *The Stone Bridge at Edobashi*, the atmosphere has a go-getting sense of bustle and the houses, like the bridge, are sturdy and utilitarian; prints in similar style display the new railway stations – and, like this one, put in some blossoming trees to indicate (truthfully enough) the continuing presence of the old Japan beneath the surface.

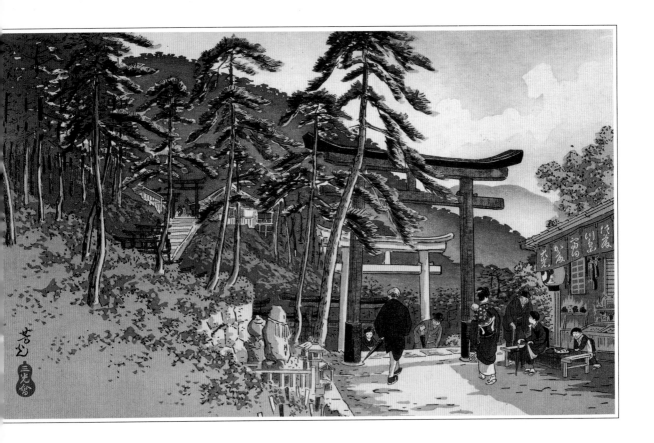

△ **Torii** 1874 Yoshimitsu (active 1870s)

TORII ARE THE GREAT carved gateways set up at the entrances to Shinto temples. The Shinto religion, unlike Buddhism, is native to Japan and is polytheistic; many of its gods and spirits are associated with specific places. The distinctively Japanese nature of the subject is ironic in view of the style in which it is executed, which represents a fairly extreme westernizing, not untypical of the early Meiji era (1868-1912); the Japanese were making their first determined efforts to overcome their economic and military inferiority after centuries of isolation and everything western – art, costume, newspapers, parliaments, locomotives – had tremendous prestige. In this pleasant, leafy view by the Osaka artist Yoshimitsu, only a single small figure suggests the alien influence by his headgear, but the entire treatment is western in its perspective and in its very un-Japanese contrasts of light and shadow.

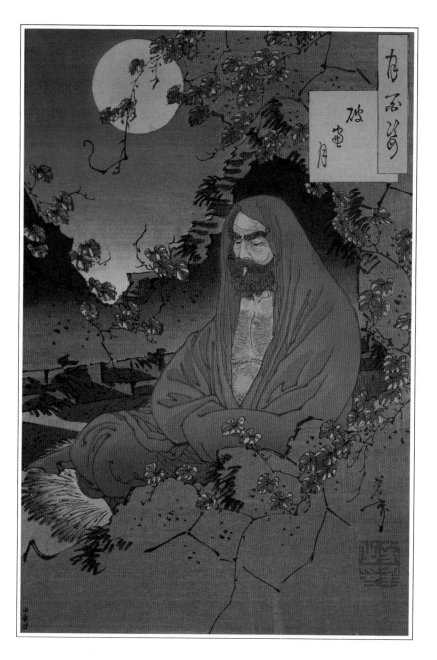

◁ **Meditation by Moonlight**
late 1880s
Yoshitoshi (1839-92)

TAISO YOSHITOSHI was the pupil of Kuniyoshi, and his work maintained much of that master's largeness and vigour while developing in a new direction. All the elements in *Meditation by Moonlight* are quite still and the scene might well come over to us as poetic and tranquil, in the style of Hiroshige. Instead, the red-shrouded, heavily bearded, contemplative figure conveys an impression of inner turbulence that is reinforced by his rocky dwelling and even by the over- large moon: we should hardly be surprised if the scene suddenly became one of violent action. Among Yoshitoshi's best works are *One Hundred Views of the Moon* and a ghost series in which his ability to disturb was at its peak. Ironically, Japan produced this highly original master of the print just when the traditional art was about to pass away.

ACKNOWLEDGEMENTS

The Publisher would like to thank the following for their kind permission to reproduce the paintings in this book:

Bridgeman Art Library, London /British Library, London: 8-9, 11, 14, 16-19, 22-24, 26-28, 32-33, 43-45, 54-55, 60, 62-63, 76; **/Private Collection:** 10, 25, 49-50, 64, 66-67, 69, 72-75, 77-78; **/British Museum, London:** 12, 30-31, 36-37, 52-53; **/Victoria & Albert Museum, London:** 13, 15, 20-21, 34, 38-39, 42, 46-48, 56-59, 70-71; **/Christie's, London:** Cover, Half-title, 35; **/Fitzwilliam Museum, University of Cambridge:** 40, 61, 65;